Business Start-up 101

Business Start-up 101

From Great Idea to Profit. . . Quick!

Chris Gattis

ISBN-13: 9781452861197
ISBN-10: 1452861196

Cover Design by: Cre8ive Partners, Huntsville, AL, www.cre8ivepartners.com
Author Picture by: Melissa Tash Studios, Huntsville, AL, www.melissatash.com

Printed in the United States of America

"Entrepreneurship is not for sissies."

- Me

Dedication

This book is dedicated to every hopeful entrepreneur who has a dream.

Worksheets

All the worksheets included in this book are for discussion and self-analysis purposes. You can find full-sized versions, MS Excel templates and other resources at **www.BusinessStartup101.com**.

Contents

Foreword

"Why is it that with all the information available today on how to be successful in small business, so few people really are?"

- Michael E. Gerber

New books about business are legion. What most of them attempt to do is, unfortunately, of little use to most of us. They are clever, or try to be. They are cute, or fail to be. They are usually about everything but what you, the beginner, need to know to take step one, step two, step three.

This book is quite different, because the author, Chris Gattis is himself quite different. He is an honest, forthright, and therefore, very dependable guide. He doesn't pretend to be anything he isn't. He is determined that you will be successful in starting up your business, by doing the things every single business owner must do, but rarely does because he or she hasn't read this book.

Yes, this book is about step one, step two, step three.
Miss the first step, and believe me, the second step will be a long way off.

Miss the second step, and you might as well go back to the very beginning.

I have personally worked with more than 70,000 small business owners throughout the world.

I met most of them after they had skipped step one and fallen on their face at step two.

I wish, now that I have read Chris Gattis' delightful and essential book, that every single one of my 70,000 plus clients had first read it before they took their first step.

Lucky you.

You now know what they didn't.

You now know what Chris Gattis set out to teach you when he began to write this book.

Business is easy, if you know the steps you need to take…and if you take each one of them, thoughtfully, carefully, intelligently.

Welcome to the wonderful world of small business!

Michael E. Gerber
Carlsbad, California

Introduction

*"Whether you think you can or think you can't,
either way you are right."*

–Henry Ford

This book is meant to be a hands-on guide. There are plenty of books on the market about business theories, marketing theories, management theories and the like. This isn't one of those books. This book is about how to start a business, from beginning to end, a step-by-step how to guide. I coach dozens of would-be entrepreneurs every month on the finer points of how to get into business and have developed and fine-tuned this strategy over the course of countless hours of discussion, studying the best practices of really good organizations and worst practices of really poor organizations.

One thing you should understand before you get started is that starting a business is not for sissies! Entrepreneurship is hard work and takes what will sometimes seem like endless hours of practice before you get it right. It will take much longer than you hope to be successful. It will take much more money than you expected before you become self-sufficient. It will take a much bigger toll on your person and family before you ever turn your venture into a self-sustaining, profit generating, hands-off organization that will return profits to you whether you are there managing it day-to-day or not. Don't say I didn't warn you!

I don't say those things to depress you or to cause you to give up on your dream, quite the contrary. I want you to do the proper planning and positioning so that you can be successful and don't become another SBA statistic. I don't want you to go into a business start-up in a half-assed way that causes you to lose your life savings or incur a giant debt that you'll be repaying for the rest of your life. You've worked and saved all your working life to get where you are now, let's don't blow it in a rush to start a business without a proper plan in place.

I'm a huge fan of Michael Gerber's entrepreneurial philosophy embodied in *The E-Myth Revisited*. I've read this and most of Michael's other books and truly believe that creating a business based on systems to take the variation out and make running the business a no-brainer. In other words, put the brain-work in up front and the business will run itself later. I believe in his philosophies so much that I asked him to write the forward to this book. I have heard Michael speak about systemizing a business; I've discussed it with him over dinner and had countless discussions with coaching and consulting clients and other coaches about taking a struggling business and creating systems to more efficiently run various parts of or the whole business. I am a full-fledged believer in utilizing this type of system to run a business. But here's the rub: you've got to get into business in a successful way to ever get to the point of needing to systemize anything.

That's what this book is all about. How you create a business that is viable. By viable, I mean it will have real customers who pay real money to buy real products or services in sufficient quantity so that your business can make real profits. To do that requires you to understand the industry in which you'll operate, the other companies against which you'll compete and the customers to which you'll sell. It also requires that you have a plan for marketing and strategies for advertising and promoting your business and products or services. This is not Hollywood nor a farm in Iowa; just because you start a business does *not* mean that customers will come. And finally, you need tools to help measure your success and fine tune your plan.

If all that planning sounds like a lot of work, it is. Can you start a business without all this planning? You bet! But there's a reason that 80 – 90% of new businesses fail, they didn't do the proper planning. Notice that I'm not talking about writing a business plan. Writing a business plan is not what's important. It's the planning that really matters. Vetting your model to ensure that it's reasonable and will return the kind of financial results that you expect is what this process is all about. If it doesn't, can you make changes to your business model so that it will give you different and better results? It's not until we get all that settled that we need to worry about writing a business plan.

The Big Idea

So you've got a great idea for a business, now what? The question you're really asking is how do you turn a great idea into money? It's the question inside the question that entrepreneurs are afraid to ask out loud. I wonder why that is? Isn't that what creating a business is all about, making a profit to support you and your family in a lifestyle you can grow accustomed? As far as I'm concerned, it is. I'm not sure why many people now consider profit a bad word. We need profit to grow businesses, hire employees and make charitable contributions. Without profit, we'd have none of that. The answer can be summed up in one word: entrepreneurship. In other words, turn your great idea into a business.

Merriam-Webster defines entrepreneurship as:

> "one who organizes, manages, and assumes the risks of a business or enterprise."

The concept that a person can take an idea and turn it into a profitable business and achieve financial security is the embodiment of the American Dream. For years, individuals have been developing ideas into businesses. Some have taken really harebrained ideas and become overnight successes. The pet rock comes to mind. It was the harebrained idea of Gary Dahl. While this business was a fluke, that is the inventor hit the market with an idea at just the right time with just the right product and just the right marketing and promotion and just the right capital to back it all up, the idea is unlikely to be repeated...or is it?

The modern day pet rock has been launched and is the must have item for all tweens. It's basically a colored rubber band that when relaxed is in the shape of well, lots of different things. Silly Bandz® are shaped like hippos, alligators, dolphins, baseballs, footballs, and most any other animal, vegetable or mineral shape you can think of. These silly things rival the pet rock for originality and uselessness, but have far surpassed it in marketing prowess and copycat appeal.

Gary Dahl was interviewed several years after the 1975 introduction of the Pet Rock and said that he had other ideas. As far as anyone knows, they were never brought to market, or more likely, the harebrained ideas were just that...harebrained ideas whose time never came.

I hope your idea has a little more merit than Pet Rocks or Silly Bandz®, because the stars really have to all be aligned for a harebrained idea to take hold and prosper. Fortunately, good ideas are turned into businesses every day. It's my job with this book to help you analyze your idea to see if it's viable so that you don't have to depend on the alignment of stars and planets.

There are all kinds of statistics from government and private sources about how many businesses survive and how many fail.

Generally speaking, roughly 80 - 90% of new businesses fail. And there's a good reason. Depending on which publication you read or which organization you believe, there are literally dozens of reasons start-ups fail. I generally categorize business failures into three groups:

1. The idea behind the business was a silly non-star aligned harebrained idea
2. The real idea behind the buisness wasn't sufficiently studied and planned
3. The individual starting the business screwed up.

In fact, operator error is the root cause of almost every business failure. The owner didn't understand the market, the capital requirements, the complexities of partnerships or the seriousness of cash flow. Oh, the cash flow, that vital nurishment of all small businesses. Perhaps the market turned sour and the owner didn't have enough capital to sustain though the bad times. Could we add a fourth category or fifth or tenth? Sure. But I generally categorize anything not a 1 or a 2 as operator error. You can make the case (it's semantics really) that the economy turning isn't something that the owner can do anything about. I could argue that the owner should have forseen lean times and had a reserve. Does it really matter?   I think you get the point.

The good news is that starting a business is not rocket science. There is a well-defined method to the madness and there are easy to use tools to help you determine if your idea is the next bread-slicer. You don't have to be a CPA to apply the financial tools either. I teach these concepts to hopeful entrepreneurs with no financial background every month. It's not that hard to get a basic understanding of business financials. You will not be sitting for the CPA exam, but you can take your business model and test whether it is financially viable and determine how much capital is needed to get it started.

If we look back to the definition of entrepreneurship, it suggests that someone is organizing and managing a business. That someone is you. It's the organizing and managing that tends to get in the way of most people being successful. That's the part that makes starting a business such a risky proposition. However, the statistic that you don't usually hear is that for people who get some business education and coaching, the statistic turns upside-down. Entrepreneurs who get business and financial education and who work with a mentor or coach tend to succeed at an 80% rate. Now that's more like it.

Enough talking about it, let's get to it.

Part 1: Entrepreneurship

*"Every business is a family business. To ignore
this is to court disaster"*

–Michael Gerber

Personal Goals

Starting a new business can be a scary proposition. Do you have what it takes? Starting a new business can be extremely time consuming and may require participation from your family or your absence from family events. Either way, you'll need your family's support and understanding and everyone should understand the goals and objectives up front.

Goals & Objectives

First, you should ask yourself why you want to start a business. Many people want to start a business for all the wrong reasons. What are your reasons?

- High Income?
- Nights & Weekends Free?
- Create income to:
  - Buy A Car?
  - Buy A Boat?
  - Buy A House?
  - Travel?
  - Hobbies?
  - Lifestyle Improvement?
  - College Education?
  - Medical Expenses?
  - Retirement Fund?

What is your goal timeline?
- o   1 Year?
- o   3 Years?
- o   5 Years?
- o   Tomorrow?

Does starting a business REALLY help you achieve your goals?

You need to clearly understand your motivation for starting a business and then decide if starting a business will help you achieve your goals. If you plan to make your fortune in a few months and start living the good life, think again. Most new business owners make little or no income for the first few years in business. In fact, many times, your employees will make more than you until your business is well established and financially stable.

Spend some time thinking about your goals. Why do you want to start a business? What do you hope to get out of it? Many would-be entrepreneurs thought that by starting a business they wouldn't have to work for the 'man' any longer. What they found was they traded one 'man' for another. The new boss is probably much harder to work for and requires significantly longer hours and a much higher quality of work than the old 'man' required.

Spend some time thinking about your motivation for wanting to start a business. Discuss your thoughts with your spouse and family. Starting a business is a family affair, whether you plan for it to be or not. While your family may not work directly in your business, they are influenced by how it affects you and your time away from home. No matter how hard you try to keep your family life and work life balanced, a new business needs lots of attention to be successful.

Personal Goals Worksheet

Honestly answer the following questions. Afterward, discuss your answers with your spouse and family members.

Why do you want to start a business?

To make o th that satisfies a customer & creates a better culture.

What do you hope to accomplish?

To bring back class.

What lifestyle are you seeking?

- Working Hours

  as many as needed

- Income

  as much as I can

- Other

Personal Financial Situation

How much cash do you need to start your business and from
where will it come? If you plan to borrow money from a bank,
credit union or other financial institution, the biggest determining
factor will be your personal credit score. If your personal credit is
not good, you may have to postpone your start-up until you can
build up your credit score or plan to get your start-up cash
elsewhere.

The personal credit score is the first and most often cited reason
that individuals are unable to borrow money to finance their
business dreams. They never get a chance to describe their idea,
show their financials or impress with their strategies. The banker
looks at the personal credit score (called a FICO Score) and says,
"No thanks."

If you will need to borrow money from a financial institution to
finance your start-up, you will need a minimum credit score of
680, and probably much higher. Make an appointment with a
commercial loan officer at your bank and discuss the process.
Find out what the bank's credit requirements are and make sure
you have a high enough credit score to qualify. While you're
there you can get a general idea of the bank's requirements and
you can find out if they lend to start-ups. Many banks and credit
unions don't lend money to start-ups at all. Your company may
need a couple of years seasoning before they will consider a
financing request. Of course, you probably won't need the money
by then. We will discuss different ways to raise start-up capital
later in the book.

Starting a business may actually hurt your personal financial
position. If you're going to borrow money personally for a new
vehicle or a home, being self-employed will create a problem if

your business is new. Retail bankers are not business bankers and may not have the skills to evaluate or understand your business. It's not their job to review your business to determine if you have the capability to repay a loan. They will want to see several years of profitable operation in the form of financial statements and tax returns. If you are unable to produce those, you will not be viewed favorably.

Let's look at some more specific questions that you'll need to consider before taking the first step to starting a new business.

1. How much cash do you have to invest in your new business?
    o   Where will it come from?
        ▪   Cash?
        ▪   Savings?
        ▪   Investment Account?
        ▪   Retirement Account?
        ▪   Home Equity?

    o   Will you have to borrow it?
        ▪   Immediate Family?
        ▪   Other Relatives?
        ▪   Friends?
        ▪   Investor?
        ▪   Financial Institution?

    Even if you do qualify to borrow start-up funds from your local bank, you will not be able to borrow the entire amount. Most banks will require you to contribute at least 10% of the start-up cash to fund your business. Generally, you should be prepared to contribute 25 – 50% of the start-up cash. The bank doesn't want to be the only cash investor in your business.

2. How long can you and your family survive without you
    providing an income?
    - o   6 Months?
    - o   1 Year?
    - o   3 Years?
    - o   Forever?

    Are you prepared to support your family with funds other
    than from your new business? You should plan on a
    minimum of 6 months and more realistically 1 – 2 years
    before your business starts returning an income.
    Depending on your level of confidence and the specific
    business model, you may have to wait much longer to start
    generating a significant salary or return on your business
    investment.

3. How much income do you realistically require?

    How much cash do you need to survive? Take some time
    to plan your family budget. You may have to reduce your
    spending in some areas of your budget. Perhaps you have
    to bring your lunch from home instead of eating out at
    noon. Maybe you bring a thermos of coffee instead of
    getting fancy Starbucks® coffee drinks. And unless you
    have lots of cash stashed away to live on, you'll probably
    decide to forgo the family vacation so that you can stay
    home and work on your new business.

4. Would you be better off financially getting a different job
    than starting a business?

    For many people, their dreams could be accomplished
    without having to start a business. Could you accomplish
    the same goals by getting a different job or trying for a

promotion at your current place of employment? Would spending an extra couple of hours a week at work give you the advantage you need to get the promotion? That might be a better strategy and one that probably has significantly less risk.

5. Would increasing your education provide you the income you desire?

    A college degree or an advanced degree might propel you to higher earning in your field. While going to college or back to college for an advanced degree is a time-consuming and difficult proposition, it's much easier and less risky than starting a business. Is a new or advanced degree all you need to accomplish your goals?

6. Have you prepared a family budget and considered your major upcoming financial obligations?
    o   New Vehicle
    o   College or Educational Expenses
    o   Medical Needs

    This is one of the most difficult parts of the evaluation process. It causes people to look harshly at their current financial position over the next few years. Will you have a child going off to college soon or need to replace a vehicle by the end of the year? Besides the money you have set aside for starting a new business, do you have at least a six month safety net of cash on hand? If not, that should be your first priority.

For some people, going to school to get a college degree or a specific technical degree or going back to school for an advanced degree will provide the increased income levels they desire without the risk associated with starting a business. For others, changing jobs or adding a part-time activity will do the trick. You should realistically consider the risk vs. reward trade-off of starting a business.

Again, this guide is not meant to stifle the entrepreneurial spirit brewing inside. It is meant to 'weed out' the people who aren't ready or don't have the resources or family support to start a business. A recent Small Business Administration statistic reflects that a whopping 95% of new employers fail in the first five years. Many of the individuals behind these businesses lost their life savings or created a gigantic debt burden that must be repaid or the burden of a personal bankruptcy when their business failed. I want you to slow down, do the proper planning and create a sufficient support structure to ensure your success.

Be honest as you explore these personal financial issues and discuss the implications with your spouse and family. Your family is a vital cog in the wheel of a new business. I've said that several times already and we're just in Part 1. You can't untie your business and your family. It's just not possible, so you'd better include them in the upfront portion of the discussion. They will be dramatically affected by the success or failure of your business and they should get a voice in the discussion.

Sources of Cash for Business Start-up Worksheet

In the worksheet below, enter the estimated amount of cash you have available to invest in a new business in the center column and the availability of that cash in the third column. Discuss your estimates with your spouse or significant other.

Source of Start-Up Funds	$ Amount	Availability
Business Owner		
Personal Checking	$ 200	now
Joint Checking w/Spouse	$ /	
Savings	$ 900	now
Investment Account	$ 1,200	3 years
Retirement Savings	$ /	
Home Equity	$ /	
Other Asset	$	
Other:	$	
Other:	$	
Total Business Owner	$ 2,300	
Family & Friends		
Name:	$	
Name:	$	
Name:	$	
Total Family & Friends	$	
Financial		
Bank:	$	
Credit Union:	$	
Investment Firm:	$	
Other:	$	
Other:	$	
Total Financial	$	
Total All Sources	$	

Personal Financial Statement

You should complete a detailed personal financial statement at least yearly. Make sure to keep a dated copy of your financial statement to compare from year-to-year. If you do not have a personal financial statement form, you can download a template form from www.businessstart-up101.com.

There are several ways to check your personal financial progress from year to year. Most people measure their financial success by their paycheck. However, you should start measuring your financial progress by using a personal financial statement. A personal financial statement does for you personally what a balance sheet does for your business. It is the truest measure of your financial stability.

Looking only at your current job income is an incomplete picuture of your financial well-being. What happens if you lose your job? How much cash reserve do you have on hand? How many monthly financial obligations do you have? How much debt have you accumulated in pursuit of your dream? A personal financial statement is the true determination of your financial success, your net worth.

Get in the habit of completing a personal financial statement every year. If you borrow money from a financial institution to fund your business start-up, it will be a required submittal. But more importantly, it's a way for you to measure yourself.

Personal Financial Statement Worksheet

In the space provided below, estimate the value of the asset (what you own) and the amount of the liability (the amount you owe) for the assets and liability categories that apply to your personal financial situation. Total the assets and liabilities. The difference between the total assets and total liabilities equals your personal net worth.

Personal Financial Statement of:

Date:

ASSETS		Liabilities & Net Worth	
Cash		Bank Loans	
Investments		Credit Card Debt	
IRA/401(k)		Consumer Loans	
Cash Value - Life Insurance		Personal Real Estate Mortgages	
Real Estate: Personal		Investment Real Estate Mortgages	
Real Estate: Investment		Loans Against Life Insurance	
Privately Owned Businesses		Other Liabilities	
Personal Assets		**TOTAL LIABILITIES**	
Other Assets			
TOTAL ASSETS		**NET WORTH**	

Preparing For Success

For you to be successful, you need a well defined strategy and a solid plan. Start from the end result you want: Success! Now work backwards identifying the key strategies that will get you to success. Define the steps involved for each strategy and create an action plan for each step. By working backwards, you can create a time-sensitive plan that allows you to meet your strategy goals and your time goals.

Your time is precious. Concentrate every day on your plan. Prioritize your activity based on accomplishing your goals. Sift through the clutter and remove from your list those activities that don't help you move your plan to the next phase. It's not about time management, it's about accomplishing goals.

Success is as much a mental state as it is a material or financial state. Consider how you will achieve your success and what sacrifices will be necessary to achieve your particular brand of success. By creating a personal vision or your rules for success, you'll be able to keep the proper balance between financial and material success as well as personal dignity and life balances. As you move forward in your career, use your rules to help you make good decisions that will guide you to the right kind of success.

Choosing the Right Business

You've decided to go into business or buy an existing business, but which one? With all the choices, how do you pick a business that suits your needs and is a good match with your skills? Think about some basic questions to help narrow your choices:

1. Your Skills – What are your skills? Are you good at engineering solutions or creative work, administrative details

or selling? Think about your specific skills and personality and how they match up against the business ideas for which you're interested.

2.   Your Interests – Maybe your interests or hobbies can be turned into a business. If your business model involves activities that you don't enjoy, maybe you should pick another business. It's got to be more than just money. If you don't enjoy what you're doing, you're unlikely to be successful.

3.   Lifestyle – What sort of lifestyle are you hoping to create for you and your family through business ownership? Be honest with yourself. Although in the beginning, you'll be working long and hard hours, in the long-term you'll hope to create a lifestyle for yourself that has certain characteristics. Discuss those characteristics with your spouse and family and make sure your business choice matches. If you're looking forward to having weekends to travel and play, don't choose to be a Realtor or open a business that does business on the weekends.

On the flipside, make sure you aren't trying to create a business out of what is essentially just a hobby. Can you really make money using your hobby or interest as the basis of a business model? The best kind of job is the kind you love; just make sure you have the basis for an actual business.

4.   Money – What sort of financial requirements do your different business choices involve? If you only have a small amount of cash to invest and don't have good prospects for borrowing more, then you need to find a business model that doesn't require a significant cash infusion. We'll discuss income statements, cash flows and investment requirements

in Part 4 of this book.

5. <u>Find Your Niche</u> – Most successful entrepreneurs started by finding a niche where they could excel. You can't hope to be everything to everybody, so find a specialty in the market and be the expert there.

6. <u>Your Personality</u> – Make sure your personality matches the business you choose. If you're shy and introverted, you probably shouldn't pick a payday loan or check cashing business. Similarly, if you're loud and obnoxious, you might not make a good grief counselor. Finding a business that fits your personality will make a huge difference in your happiness with the choice down the road.

7. <u>Your Location</u> – If you live in the mountains, starting a water skiing instruction business may not make sense. If you live in the desert, scuba diving may not be the right business for you. Organic gardening might be an excellent choice in some areas, but not in a busy city. A bicycle delivery service is going to struggle in a rural farming community. Use a little common sense when thinking about your location and how that affects the businesses that you are considering. Also, think about your customers and how your location or their location might affect your ability to deliver your product or service to them.

8. <u>The Idea</u> – Is your idea viable? Do a reality check with your business advisors. Utilize the *Three Tools of Financial Viability*™ in section four to determine if your business model will generate sufficient income and cash flow and will break-even at a reasonable level. Does the model create enough profit to justify the amount of time and effort required to

generate it?

9.   <u>Take Your ime</u> – You need to get this right and it doesn't
     make sense to jump into something quickly just to make a
     decision. Think about starting something on a part-time basis
     to make sure you're really committed and interested. Talk to
     your advisors, friends and family and get their take on your
     ideas. Don't feel rushed into a decision. Take your time and
     get it right.

Don't let skeptical friends and associates talk you out of starting a
business just because they are risk averse. Most people are not cut
out to be entrepreneurs. Do carefully consider any objections or
constructive criticism of your plan. Evaluate the feedback and
then move on based on your analysis. At the end of the day, it's
you who will be starting the business, not your friends.

Personal Interest Worksheet

Describe your skills.

- Making things
- Close to perfection things

What lifestyle characteristics do you desire from your business?

- Simple but elegant

What are your interests and hobbies that might be used in a business?

- classic clothing (bow ties ect.)
- classic cars
- shooting

Describe your personality traits.

- mostly introverted, but can be a people person, when the need arrives.
- inovative
- unique ideas to fix problems

Are you cut out to be an entrepreneur?

Some people are born entrepreneurs and others have to learn the skills. Anyone can learn the skills if they are willing to invest the time and energy to do so. Answer the following questions honestly using a 1 through 5 scale where 5 is *I completely agree* and 1 is *I completely disagree.*

_4_ **1. Are you self-motivated?** Do you push yourself to be the best you can be and get as much done each day as possible? Are you willing to work the long hours necessary to get a business started? In the beginning, it may feel like you're working 24/7. Do you jump out of bed in the morning to begin your day or does your spouse have to drag you out by your feet? Starting a business requires self-motivation, as there's no one else to give you that kick in the backside to get going. It also requires a significant amount of energy. You have to be the head cheerleader for your business motivating your employees, vendors and customers to your cause.

_5_ **2. Does your family support your venture?** You don't go into business alone. Your family and friends are there with you, either voluntarily supporting and cheering you on or involuntarily dragging you down and throwing one roadblock after another in front of you. The decision to start a business should be a family decision. Of course you have to make the final decision, but you should include your family or significant other and maybe even your friends to ensure that you have their support and encouragement. You're going to need all the help and support you can get in the first couple of years. Starting off in a fight with your family about your absence or distraction is no way to begin.

_3_ **3. Do you play well with others?** As a business owner, you'll be interacting with customers who are difficult and demand the unreasonable. You'll be negotiating with vendors who are charging too much. You'll be discussing salary and benefits with your employees and partners. Can you have tense and sometimes difficult discussions without losing your cool? Can you bargain with vendors and salespeople without being emotional? Do you know when to push people's buttons and when to leave well enough alone? How will you handle rejection after the 20th unsuccessful sales call?

_3_ **4. Do you have any experience in business?** You don't have to be Bill Gates or Warren Buffett, but you should have some idea how the business world works. If you've never been higher up in an organization than drive thru operator, you should consider getting some business experience prior to jumping in feet first. All the skills needed to run a successful business can be learned. Just make sure to take the time to actually learn them prior to pouring your 401(k) into a new venture.

_5_ **5. Can you sell yourself?** As owner of your new business, you have to constantly be selling your products and services. But even more importantly, you have to sell yourself. If you don't believe in yourself and what you're doing, how do you expect others to buy in? Especially in the beginning, you can't depend on some non-existent sales force to create interest and orders. You have to sell yourself and your business. If you can't do this, you should seriously reconsider going into business for yourself.

Add your scores from the five questions.

MY SCORE $\boxed{21}$

If you scored less than...

10   You may not be cut out for entrepreneurship. Consider
              your motivation for business ownership carefully. Could
              you create similar results by finding another employment
              opportunity? Maybe you should consider keeping your
              activity a hobby, rather than full-time employment. If you
              still have that entrepreneur spark burning, you'll have to
              devote more time and effort to learning the skills necessary
              to be successful.

If you scored between...

11 - 19   You have some definite traits of an entrepreneur, but you
              need to continue to develop your business, leadership and
              sales skills. Shortcomings in entrepreneurial skills can be
              overcome with education and study. Shortcomings in
              personality and demeanor are much more difficult to
              change. Consider your motivation carefully and discuss
              your plans with your family. Have your spouse or other
              family member grade you independently and together
              devise an education plan to help you move forward.

If you scored more than...

20   You are a born entrepreneur. Continue to develop your
              plan and get ready for success!

Part 2: Business Management

"The best way to get a good idea, is to get a lot of ideas."

−Linus Pauling

If you're still with me, it's time to start building your business. I tend to lose a bunch of people after the first section when they realize that starting a business really is going to be hard work. I try to make that very clear up front. I also try to make it clear that you have to do careful planning and research to ensure that your efforts are rewarded with success. If you'll just do your homework and use the tools that I'll outline later in the book, you can be successful.

I'm going to start off by discussing some of the more mechanical parts of starting a business. These ideas have more to do with starting and running a physical business entity. After that we'll begin our business planning and forming our business model to ensure that it's viable and successful.

Accounting & Accounting Systems

Accounting Method

There are two accounting methods for a small business: cash and accrual. A cash accounting method is best used for a sole proprietorship or extremely small business with no employees. A cash system accounts for the activity of the business as cash is paid out or received into the business. For example, a sale is not recorded as a sale until payment of the invoice is received. The big advantage of this system is the accounting entries are very easy and straightforward. The biggest disadvantage is that the business cycle of sales, collections and payments to vendors tend to happen in hunks and don't represent a smooth flow of reporting.

An accrual system is based on recording business activity when the activity happens, not necessarily when the cash changes hands. For example, when you invoice a customer for a sale, you record the transaction as a sale in the accounting system. When the customer pays the invoice, you record the cash receipt. When you receive a vendor invoice, you record the payable in your accounting system and then you record the payment of the invoice only when you actually write the check. While this system requires many more accounting entries to record the business cycle, the cycle smoothing makes the financial statements *look* more accurate. We'll discuss more about how those looks can be deceiving in Part 4.

In reality, most businesses use a hybrid system that includes some cash and some accrual methods. And for most small businesses, that's not a real problem. If you don't have accounting expertise on staff, you can hire a part-time employee, temporary employee or engage an outside firm to maintain your regular bookkeeping duties. In any case, you should be using an outside accounting firm with CPA oversight to prepare your official year end statements and help you prepare your tax returns. A good accountant will make the proper adjusting entries to get your books in line with accounting standards that the IRS expects for tax reporting purposes.

For everyday use, it's important that you record your business activity consistently. That is, don't change the way you report your activity unless advised to do so by your accountant, and then consistently do it the way you have been advised.

Regular recording of transactions in your accounting system is critical to stay on top of your business performance and manage your finances and cash. Depending on your level of business activity, a small business can usually get by with a few hours a week to a few hours a month of bookkeeping activity. Hiring an outside bookkeeper or service is a good way to keep your costs low but still get the reporting information that you need to properly manage your business.

Recordkeeping

Managing your business records is not only an important management function of your business, but a requirement of the Internal Revenue Service. There are as many ways to keep up with business information as there are people doing it. The important thing is to set up a system that works for you and your business and do it consistently. If you're not interested in setting up a recordkeeping system for your business, you probably shouldn't go into business in the first place. It's these details of running a business that tend to trip up entrepreneurs who are more interested in making the next deal or marketing campaign. And while all that is good and necessary to keeping a business going, the details are what let you know if you're making money, running out of cash or headed for an imminent train wreck.

But what sort of records should you keep? The type of business you operate will dictate exactly what types of records you keep. However, the following categories will apply to most companies and can serve as a guide to the types of records you should maintain. You should maintain and keep the supporting documents that show the amounts and sources of income or expense in the following catgegories:

Sales
- Cash register tapes
- Bank deposit slips

- Receipt books
- Invoices
- Credit card charge slips

You'll need some method to capture sales information. If you are in a retail environment, you may have a point-of-sale register that records information about your cash sales that can be downloaded into a bookkeeping system or printed for use in tax reporting preparation. Either way, you'll need to track your transactions not just for sales tax reporting, but for general business intelligence and performance measurement.

If you're selling on open account, you'll need a system that takes your point-of-sale transactions and reports the data in an accounts receivable system.

If you are selling in a wholesale environment, you'll need to document when you do and do not charge sale taxes. A system of collecting tax resale certificates, tax exemption certificates and direct payment permits by customer and job is typically required by the local and state taxing authorities. Train your sales and customer service employees to ask the customer about the taxable nature of the transaction and to which job the purchase corresponds so that you can help each other keep the records straight and everyone in compliance. It is almost impossible to recreate these records after the fact.

Purchases

- Canceled checks
- Cash register tape receipts
- Credit card sales slips
- Invoices
- Packing slips
- Shipping orders

- Purchase Orders

Any purchases you make for your business will require backup documentation that reflects the details of the transaction and the business purpose of the purchase.

Expenses

- Canceled checks
- Cash register tapes
- Account statements
- Credit card sales slips
- Invoices
- Petty cash slips for small cash payments

Travel and entertainment expenses must document who attended the meal or event, the business purpose, and the date and time. Documentation can be done right on the sales slip, credit card receipt or a separate attached document.

Accounting Systems

In order to properly manage and account for your business activity, you'll need some sort of system to keep track of your transactions. For a very small business, you can use a paper system or even a spreadsheet type arrangement to keep track of your business activity. However, if your business is of any size, you'll need a more robust system of accounting.

The most common system in use by small business is Intuit's QuickBooks. The beauty of utilizing QuickBooks is that it operates in the same way you operate your business. You create invoices, pay bills, make deposits and so forth. The system handles the accounting in the background. That's not to say that you can buy the program and be an expert immediately. While the system works great for most small business, it does require some experience to get it set up properly.

Most communities have QuickBooks consultants or accounting firms that will help you get your company set up and running in QuickBooks so that you or your employees can handle the daily, weekly and monthly entries required to properly manage your business. If your business is very small, you can utilize what I call the "shoe-box accounting method." That is, you collect all the receipts and transactional information each week or month, depending on the size of your business, and hand it off to an accountant who will make the entries into your system. After the entries are made, the accountant will typically give you a set of reports that reflect the profitability and cash position of your business.

The "shoe-box method" is an acceptable method for very small businesses, but one that should not be utilized for a business of any size for an extended length of time. As a small business owner, you need to have an intimate understanding of how what you do in the business world affects your profitability and cash flow. In fact, as the owner, you shouldn't go to bed at night without having a firm grasp of your cash situation. That means, how much cash you have on hand, as well as what your cash requirements and cash collection expectations are for at least the next week.

When you first start you business, you may have a hard time understanding the relationship of business activity to profitability and cash flow. However, if you study your financial reports and monitor your cash flow, you'll grow to understand this relationship and get better and better at managing it. You *must* get better and better at managing it. This is one of the critical skills needed for your small business success.

Whether you hire an employee to manage the data entry and accounting duties, or utilize an outside consultant or accountant, you are still responsible for creating and managing this system. You can hire out the bookkeeping work, but you still have responsibility for understanding the results and making changes to your business as the results may indicate. If you don't have the necessary skills for this function, get them. Take financial management classes at your local community college, seek out a seminar for non-financial managers or read a book. As with any professional skill, there are ways to acquire or improve your expertise. Especially in a small business, you can't give this responsibility to anyone else. If you don't care enough to understand your financial position and properly manage your buisness, who will?

Management Systems

Systems are the key to business start-up success, especially with a single owner or a small group of people. Who is in charge? Who does what? How will conflicts be arbitrated? You may be friends when you start, but without proper management systems, you'll be bitter enemies by tomorrow. However, if you have employees or partners or both, then the equation becomes a little more difficult. Creating systems and management hierarchy up front will ease many of the disputes that will otherwise arise.

Organizational Structure

One of the best ways to organize a business and manage the future conflicts up-front is to create an organization chart for your business. When you are a new business, there's usually not much organization to chart.

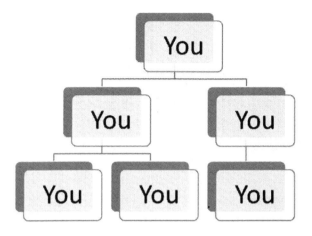

Probably the most difficult decision to make if you have partners in your business is who is in charge. Resist the temptation to jointly co-manage the business. While you and your partner or partners will obviously all participate in the decision-making, someone has to ultimately make decisions when disputes arise. In other words, who will be the President or CEO? Think about the skills and personalities that each person brings to the organization. Some are best suited for some roles and not others. Be honest with each other and yourself and create a structure that best utilizes the skills and personalities of each person.

Different types of organizations need different types of structures. A complex manufacturing operation might require a function for sales, operations (manufacturing), research and development, and administration. A service organization might only require a sales, operations and administration function. How many functions, how many levels, how flat or how tall your organization becomes is up to you. The key is to structure your organization so that it will function efficiently based on your growth plans. Imagine how your organization will look in five years. Now create a structure to support that image. Then, plug in the names of your current owners, managers and employees into those slots. Remember, you may be managing two functions and eight jobs today, but that will change over time.

Think about what you want your business to look like three to five years down the road. Create a business structure today of how you want your business to function in the future. Granted, your name will fill many of the squares on the initial organization chart, but the point is that the structure is established and as you add partners or employees, they can be placed into a box and everyone understands the responsibilities for that position.

This exercise becomes much more than an exercise if you have a partner or partners helping in the business start-up. Which partner will handle which function? Who will handle sales and who will handle accounting? Much more important than that is who will serve as president of the organization and who will serve in the other management roles. It's very important to have identified who will do what in your new business. You can't have two presidents. It just will not work. Someone has to be the ultimate decider of key issues if you can't decide together.

These issues should be settled in the beginning when everyone loves each other. Once you're in the heat of the battle is not the time to first be thinking about your management structure. Also understand that the individuals who are helping you manage the business should be assigned roles based on their, and your, skills. If you are really good with people and not much for details, then maybe one of your partners should handle the administrative duties while you concentrate on sales. And don't let percent of ownership be a detriment to making good management decisions. If you own 80% and your partner owns 20%, but they make a much better president than you, then maybe they should serve as president. Remember, the object is to create a management structure that ensures success. You are trying to build a financially viable organization and shouldn't let your personal ego get in the way of that goal. If one of your primary goals isn't to create a financially viable organization, then you should probably revisit your business model and mission statement. It's fine to have an organization that helps people or does good in the community or the world, but if you don't have a financially viable organization, how will you ever have the money to do good works?

This idea of a company that does good works in the community being at odds with making money is one I run across frequently. The business owner of a 'good works' company somehow thinks that talking about and encouraging money making and profitability is at odds with the nature of the business. Nothing could be further from the truth. In fact, just the opposite is true. If your 'good works' company doesn't make significant profits to fund those good works, how will you continue to support your work for the poor or needy or uneducated? You can't! The only way to continue your philanthropic activities is to make money. Don't think of money making as a bad thing.

The same idea holds for non-profits. Just because you are classified as a 'not for profit' business, does not mean you don't need to make money. The accounting is slightly different for a non-profit business. We don't call 'profit' profit, but that doesn't mean that we don't have to make a profit. If you don't make a 'profit', you can't stay in business. In fact, the level of services you can provide in a non-profit business is directly related to how much 'profit' you generate. If you don't generate 'profit', you don't provide service.

Review the sample organization chart on the next page and complete the worksheet. This idea of creating an organization chart for a successful company in the future will also serve as a goal and a physical reminder of where you are headed.

One of the ways I like to encourage successful thinking in
potential entrepreneurs is to think about your potential
organization as it might exist in the future if you are very
successful. In your minds eye, think about what your
organization would look like if all your dreams came true. Think
about the physical location, the employees, the contracts or work,
the look and smell of your office and feeling of that success. Now
write down what you see. Every detail should be documented
and used as an encouragement of what will come. Use this
success visioning to create an organization chart for your
successful future company. Create a chart of all the functions that
you'll need in your future organization. Draw all the boxes and
include the function name for each area. Once you're finished,
plug into this future organization chart the names of your start-up
employees, even if they are only you.

This exercise serves two purposes:

1. It serves as a goal for your organization. Look at it
    on a regular basis or post it in a picture frame and
    hang it on your wall so you can see it every day.
    Like other written goals, the mere act of writing it
    down will help it come true.
2. It serves as a structure on which to build your
    current business. True, you will not need all those
    functions on day one. However, if you start
    building your business today with your future
    success in mind, with the systems necessary for
    success, you'll not have nearly the growing pains
    or interruptions of service that many businesses
    face as they grow without the proper plans.

Example Organization Chart

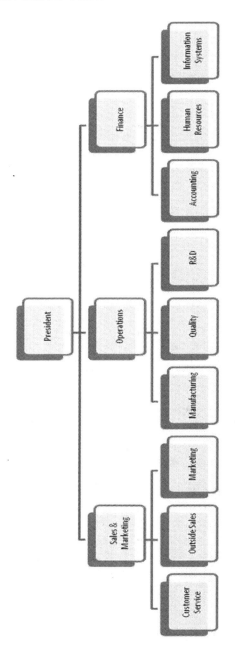

Organization Chart Worksheet

Create an organization chart for your business as it will look in five years. Enter the function name and discuss with your partners or advisors. After creating the proper structure, assign a name to each function, even if your name is in every box.

Hiring Employees

In most parts of the country, anyone with a job opening is fair game for a deluge of job applications. During times of economic hardship and high unemployment, applications will pour in from prospective employees who are grossly over-qualified to those who are wholly unqualified. Especially in times of economic hardship, there are lots of people looking for those few good jobs that become available. Hiring good people is a difficult challenge whether you have hundreds of applicants or only a couple. To help ensure that you hire the right person for the job, you'll need a hiring system to identify the work to be done, identify the person with the right skills and attitude for the job, and create the right environmnent in which the person will work.

<u>Job Description</u>

Start by identifying what you want the person to do. Craft a job description that not only identifies tasks to be completed and areas to be managed, but also identify the expected outcomes. All too often employers will hire an individual for a position but never let the person know what they expect. Then when the employee inevitably does not perform to expectations, everyone is unhappy.

Get input on job descriptions and expected performance from the person or people currently performing the job. If you've never done the job yourself, how could you possibly know the best way to do it? Also, try to find the best practices for this type of work. Create positions with challenging work and then train the individual you hire to properly perform the work. Give the employee the necessary training and other resources needed to successfully perform. Don't forget to give the employee the authority needed to properly perform the work.

Eliminate Ridiculous Hiring Practices

If you want to compete with the giants for the very best employees, streamline your hiring process and make it employee friendly. Most employee hiring systems are fraught with ridiculous requirements and cumbersome steps. While huge companies need a robust software system for sorting out the thousands of applications they get daily, small companies don't. Think of potential employees as potential customers. How would you manage this system if these were customers rather than employees? I'll bet you wouldn't create a system with 28 steps just to make an application. I'll bet you wouldn't have them come in for an interview and then not communicate with them again for 30 or 45 days. Whoever created the systems in use by most large companies today clearly wasn't interested in recruiting the best people. Which excellent employee prospect, with lots of opportunities and plenty of competition would pick your company with this stupid system? If you treat them as mindless robots before you hire them, how much worse will it be once they become actual employees?

Create an application system that's convenient for the applicant but still gets you the information you need to cull the best applicants. You're not going to make a final hiring decision based on your on-line application alone, so don't build a system that assumes you will. I heard a college admissions administrator tell of high school students trying to fill out 12-page admissions applications on an iPhone. Start thinking about your employees as the key to your business success before you ever hire them.

Set a realistic resume acceptance time and stick to it. As you cull applicants, let them know they are not being considered. As soon as the time expires, pick the ones you want to interview and get them in. If you need a second interview, schedule it within a week of completing the first interview process. Don't tell me that you or your people are busy and we can't seem to get the interviews scheduled. Do you need employees or not? If you do, make it a priority. Make a decision and extend the offer. The entire process shouldn't take more than 75 days and in many cases can be done in 30 – 45 days. If you don't find a suitable candidate, tell them so and start over.

Attitude is Everything

Especially for a start-up company, employee attitude is very important. You'll need to serve your customers quicker, be more responsive, handle complaints better, and generally jump higher and faster than your competition in order to get your business off the ground. Having employees with a 'can do' attitude and service orientation will make a huge difference. In most cases, you can train for the specific skills you need if you have an employee with the right attitude. On the flip side, you'll have a hard time getting a generally negative person with great skills to properly service your customer. It can be done, but I find it's much more difficult to train for attitude than is it to train for skills.

Don't Pay Too Much

Pay a competitive rate for the job at hand. Jacking up the pay rate will only lower your profitability and won't necessarily get you the best people. It will mostly get you people who are motivated by money. While that's not necessarily bad, it's not necessarily good either. Wanting more money is a trait found in every worker, not just good workers. Over a period of time, exceptional employees can be rewarded and paid commensurate to their value.

Retaining Employees

Hiring employees is only half of the equation. You need to keep them happy and engaged in the processes of success in order for your business to grow and prosper.

Communicate the Plan

 Nothing is worse for an employee than to be completely in the dark about the company goals and objectives and plans for getting somewhere. They don't have to know every detail, but do inform them about your latest strategic planning and how it will affect the direction of the company. Employees know when you're working on plans and they just want to know what's going on.

Make sure every employee has a physical copy or at the very least access to your mission and value statement. We will discuss developing a mission statement in Part 3 of this book. Explain to every new employee how this moral and business directive should affect how they make decisions, engage the customer, interact with vendors and how it affects the way they do their job. This core company value statement is a powerful tool for communication with your employees. All people want to be part of something grand and visionary. Make sure they behave according to your core values and reward excellence in achieving those values.

Engage People in the Process

Good employees want to feel like they are making a difference in their company. In a giant company, it will never happen. But in a small company, you can create an environment where your employees can be part of the process, not just a cog in the process wheel. As you discuss the work of your company and its different departments, get your employees involved in designing the work, the systems and the improvement processes. Create a feedback or suggestion system that actually considers employee ideas. You don't have to implement every idea that an employee has, but if you give ideas careful consideration and involve the employee in the feedback, discussion loop, and the feasibility analysis, they'll be thrilled.

Allow Employees to Take Pride in Their Work

While this may sound simplistic, it's difficult to achieve. Create an environment where employees feel like they matter. Your people want to be part of a company with a grand plan and a vision, and they want to feel like they have a vital role in helping your company achieve those goals. Your job is to create a company like that, hire good people and then don't behave stupidly. Almost all employees want to take pride in their work. Some will say they're just in it for the money, and while that may be true on some level, they also want to take pride in their work and their company. If they can't, over time they'll get tired of you and your company and find work elsewhere.

Get Out of the Way

You've spent several months hiring just the right person with the right attitude and have complete confidence in their ability to manage the function for which they were hired. Now, get out of their way and let them do their job. Don't look over their shoulder and second guess every decision. Don't micromanage a good employee into submission. If you didn't think they could do the job, why did you hire them in the first place? As an employee, it is very frustrating being micromanaged by an owner or other manager who doesn't have a clue how to do the job you were hired to do. Don't be one of those managers or owners.

Employees vs. Contractors

Many businesses try to hire workers as independent contractors to avoid the hassles of documenting, paying benefits and withholding payroll taxes. While in some cases this may be perfectly acceptable, in most cases, it is not. The IRS has even published a Top 10 List of things a small business owner should know about hiring individuals as independent contractors versus employees. Allow me to paraphrase:

Generally, the IRS uses three characteristics to determine the relationship between businesses (independent contractors) and workers: Behavioral Control, Financial Control, and the Type of Relationship. Behavior Controls refer to whether the business has the right to direct or control how the work is done through instructions, training or other means. Financial Control relates to whether the business has a right to direct or control the financial and business aspects of the worker's job. And the Type of Relationship factor relates to how the workers and the business owner perceive their relationship.

If you have the right to control or direct not only what is to be done, but also how it is to be done, then your workers are most likely employees. If you can control only the result of the work, not the means and methods of accomplishing the result, then your workers are probably independent contractors.

Employers who misclassify workers as independent contractors can end up with substantial tax bills. Additionally, they can face penalties for failing to pay employment taxes and for failing to file required tax forms.

By completing assignments as independent contractors instead of as employees, workers lose any potential company benefits such as health insurance and access to retirement accounts. An independent contractor also is required to pay self-employment tax, something not required of employees*. Workers can avoid higher tax bills and lost benefits if they know their proper status.

If you are in doubt as to whether your work can be done as an employee or independent contractor, contact your CPA or the IRS. The IRS will help you to make a determination on whether a specific individual is an independent contractor or an employee by filing a Form SS-8: Determination of Worker Status for Purposes of Federal Employment Taxes and Income Tax Withholding. Both the employer and employee can make this request.

*NOTE: The company is required to pay the matching social security tax for employees, but it does not get deducted from the employee's paycheck.

Legal Entities

THE INFORMATION PRESENTED IN THIS SECTION IS FOR EDUCATIONAL AND DISCUSSIONS PURPOSES ONLY AND SHOULD NOT BE CONSTRUED AS LEGAL ADVICE. THE AUTHOR IS NOT AN ATTORNEY AND IS NOT QUALIFIED TO GIVE LEGAL ADVICE.

There are several types of business forms, known as 'entities'. Apart from the Sole Propietorship, the business entity is a separate legal venture, different from you personally. While there are many different types of business entities, we will discuss the most common forms used today.

When you start a business, two outcomes are possible. You can be successful and your business will generate profits or your business can fail and lose money. In either event, success or failure, having the proper business structure will ensure you'll be better off. Keep in mind, for a small business, legal structures are as much about taxes as they are about legal liability. Make sure to consult with your tax advisor and attorney before selecting a legal structure.

There are three key issues to consider when deciding between different legal structures; liability, taxes and administrative costs.

Liability – Who is responsible for the debts of the business? What happens if your business is sued by a customer who is injured using one of your products or misuses your business advice and suffers a big loss? Depending on the legal structure you select, you may or may not be liable for the debts of your business.

Taxes – Taxes will be paid on business profits either by the company or if the entity is a pass-through, by the owners. In a standard corporation, taxes are paid on the profits of the business before dividends are paid to the owners. Once dividends are received by the owners, the dividends are taxed on the owner's personal return. This is what is known as double taxation. If the corporation has a loss, it doesn't have taxes, but there is no ability of the owners to utilize the loss to offset other personal incomes either. In a pass-through entity, any profits or losses are reported on the owner's individual tax returns. That way profits are only taxed once and losses can be used to offset other income.

Administrative Costs – How much does it cost in terms of dollars and more importantly, your time, to run your business? Some legal entity structures are more cumbersome and time consuming than others. Especially in the case of start-up businesses, the costs of some structures can be overwhelming to an already overworked owner.

We'll look at how the basic structures work.

 ## Sole Proprietorship

A sole proprietorship is a for-profit business owned and operated by an individual, acting as the sole owner and decision maker of a business. In a sole proprietorship, there is no difference between the business and the business owner. It is the simplest form of business entity. It is a form in which an individual conducts business in his or her own name or under a trade name rather than as a separate legal business entity. There are no formal requirements involved in forming a sole proprietorship, nor are there requirements for operations. However, you will likely still need to obtain a business license from your city, county and state and you may need to file a fictitious business name statement with the city and/or county.

Advantages:

- Easy to setup and low administrative burden
- Few regulatory requirements
- Owner is taxed on personal tax return for profits and losses of business

Disadvantages:

- Owner is personally liable for debts of the business
- Borrowing money for the business is difficult

- Owner is personally responsible for legal issues of business

The sole proprietorship business form offers no legal liability protection as any liability of the business extends against personal assets of the sole proprietor. This means that liabilities, debts, and judgments against the business can attach to the personal assets of the sole proprietor including personal bank accounts, cars and homes. Owners can sometimes purchase insurance to protect against legal liabilities.

 General Partnership

A partnership is an association of two or more persons to carry on a business for profit, as co-owners, and is characterized by a community of interests in a particular business and sharing of profits. It is similar to a sole proprietorship for multiple owners. That is, it is not a separate legal entity from its owners. The term "persons" includes individuals, partnerships, corporations, limited liability partnerships and other associations. While a general partnership is easy to form from a legal standpoint, it is also one of the least used types of partnership.

Advantages:

- Easy to setup and low administrative burden
- Few regulatory requirements
- Owner is taxed on personal tax return for profits and losses of business

Disadvantages:

- Owners are personally liable for the debts of the company

- Each partner is responsible for the business dealings of the other partners
- Partners are personally liable for legal issues of business

A general partnership is governed by the partnership agreement. While this document, in theory, can be simple to create, it has far ranging legal and operating consequences for the partners and should be crafted carefully and with legal advice. It will cover items such as initial investment contributions of the partners, how profits and losses will be distributed, the responsibilities of the partners, when and how partners can enter and exit the business.

Limited Liability Partnership

A Limited Liability Partnership is similar to a General Partnership except that there are two classifications of partners: general and limited. General partners have operational control of the business and have individual liability for the debts and actions of the partners. Limited partners are treated like investors. They have no operational control of the business and have only limited liability for the debts and actions of the business.

Advantages:

- Owner is taxed on personal tax return for profits and losses of business
- Liability can be limited for some partners

Disadvantages:

- Filing and administrative costs are more complex than a general partnership

- General partners have personal liability for debts and actions of the company

A general partnership works well if you have numerous passive investors who wish to limit their personal liability.

 Corporations

A corporation is treated as a separate and distinct legal entity, existing apart and recognized separately from its owners and shareholders, with all the rights to own property, make contracts, and sue in its own name. A corporation may be formed to engage in any business activity, subject to compliance with applicable laws. Unless specifically provided in its Articles of Incorporation, corporations are perpetual. That is, the corporation continues after the death, disability, retirement or termination of a shareholder, director or officer. A corporation is formed by filing Articles of Incorporation with the Secretary of State. Owners of the corporation are issued stock certificates representing the shares of stock issued by the corporation. Corporations may have a single owner or be owned by any type of entity. Bylaws typically set forth the rules and procedures that govern the management of a corporation. Corporations must follow strict statutory compliance in connection with meetings and record keeping. Management of the corporation's business is exercised by or under the direction of a Board of Directors.

Personal liability is limited to the extent of a shareholder's investment in the corporation. Corporate shareholders, directors and officers are not liable for the debts and other obligations of the corporation or for the torts or criminal acts of one another.

Advantages

- No personal liability for shareholders (owners)
- Ownership can be easily exchanged between individuals
- Company existence not tied to life of owners
- Easy to raise capital or borrow money

Disadvantages:

- Profits are taxed twice
- Administrative costs and setup burden is higher than other structures
- Regulatory burden can be higher than other structures

A regular corporation or "C" corporation is a separate tax-paying entity for federal and state tax purposes. Corporations are also subject to double taxation. That is, profits of the corporation are taxed to the corporation and again to the shareholders when after-tax profits are distributed to the shareholders as dividends. Corporations may raise capital through equity capital contributions by its shareholders or loans secured by its assets.

 Subchapter S Corporation

A subchapter S corporation, commonly referred to as an "S corporation", is a corporation that has elected to be taxed under Subchapter S of the Internal Revenue Code and is treated as a partnership for most tax purposes. Thus, the income and losses of the S corporation are proportionately passed through to its shareholders, who report and pay taxes on their individual tax returns. Other than the different tax treatment and ownership qualifications, S corporations operate identically to a C corporation.

Advantages:

- Owners pay taxes on their individual tax returns
- Shareholders (owners) are not personally liable for the debts and activities of company

Disadvantages:

- Administrative costs and setup burden is higher than other structures
- Regulatory burden can be higher than other structures
- Limitations of who can be an owner

An S corporation may have no more than 75 shareholders who generally are all U.S. citizen individuals, estates and certain types of trusts. They must be U.S. corporations and may not issue more than one class of stock. Other rules for certain types of obscure corporate operations may also apply.

 Limited Liability Companies

A Limited Liability Company (LLC) is an entity having one or more members, organized under a particular state statue. The owners of an LLC are called members rather than shareholders. LLCs are recognized in all 50 states and may engage in any lawful business activity allowed by their Articles of Organization. However, not all states allow a single-member LLC. Unless statutorily prohibited in a particular state, members of an LLC may be individuals, trusts, and other business entity types, including foreign individuals and entities. The LLC may be managed by all of its members or by one or more managers appointed by the members.

An LLC with two or more members may elect to be taxed as either a corporation or a partnership. A single member LLC may elect to be taxed as a corporation or be disregarded as an entity separate from its owner. State tax treatment is specific to the state.

Advantages:

- Owners pay taxes on their individual tax returns
- Members are not personally liable for debts and activities of company
- Ease of change to structure

Disadvantages:

- Higher administrative costs and setup than partnership or sole proprietorship
- More regulations than partnership or sole proprietorship
- LLC laws are state specific and not uniform

LLCs are extremely popular legal structures due to their ease of setup and pass-through tax structure. In addition, changes to the management structure or operations are as simple as making a change in the Operating Agreement or filing an amendment to the Articles of Organization.

Local Requirements

Employer Identification Number

While not a local requirement, most businesses need an Employer Identification Number or EIN. If you hire employees or have anything other than a sole proprietorship, you need an EIN. The process is simple and can be completed on-line at www.irs.gov.

"Incorporation" Papers

Depending on your business entity type, you'll need to file the organization papers with the State. Exactly what kind of paperwork needs to be filed depends on the type of business entity you are creating and the state of incorporation. Contact the Secretary of State office or your attorney for the details.

Business Privilege Tax

Many states require some sort of privilege tax for any corporation, partnership or LLC. The tax is typically paid yearly and may or may not be based on your gross receipts.

State/County Business License

You'll need a business license when you open your business. The fees are generally small for a new business and can be handled through the county license office.

City Business License

If your business is located in the city limits, you'll need a city business license. If you do business in other cities, you'll need to get a business license for each of those cities as well. The penalties can be harsh for not getting a license and at the least you'll get shut down until the process is completed to the local cities satisfaction. And yes, it can get burdensome.

Sales Tax Reporting

If your business sells anything other than services, you'll need to collect, report and pay sales tax on those transactions. Depending on your location, you may have to report to the state, county and municipality for any sales you make.

<u>Use Tax Reporting</u>

If your business buys products or services on-line or from vendors out of state and the product is shipped via U. S. Postal Service or a common carrier, you'll need to report those transactions to the city, county and state so you can be charged use tax. Use tax is just sales tax that wasn't collected on a transaction because of the method of delivery or location of the seller. Out of state and many on-line transactions don't charge sales tax. That doesn't mean sales tax isn't due. It's just your responsibility to report those transactions and pay the tax. If you're thinking of ignoring those transactions, remember that a sales tax audit also includes Use Tax reporting.

<u>Special Permits</u>

Depending on your business, you may need any number of special permits from the local authorities. In general, the following activities may require a special permit:

- Food Service
- Alcohol Sales
- Taxicabs, Limousines & Carriage Service
- Building & Construction Trades
- Gaming & Bingo
- Event Hosting
- Historical Properties
- Drilling & Mineral Rights
- Pyrotechnics & Blasting
- Firearm Sales & Distribution
- Hazardous Chemicals Handling

If your business will be involved in any of these trades or other areas that are typically highly regulated, you'll probably need a permit.

<u>Planning & Zoning</u>

Plan Commission and Zoning Board permission may be required if you intend to operate your business in a part of the city or county where those activities are not permitted. For example, a manufacturing operation will not be allowed to operate out of a property zoned for any kind of residential use. This is an extreme example to make a point. Frequently the uses and permissions are not nearly so clear cut. If in doubt, check with your local city or county officials. This is **not** an area where begging forgiveness is better than asking permission.

Intellectual Property

Intellectual property refers to inventions, product or process improvements, works of authorship such as writing and music, artistic work, designs, images, formulations and names. The owners of these assets need to protect their unauthorized use. Intellectual Property is divided into four categories: Patents, Trademarks, Copyrights and Trade Secrets. If you are unsure of your rights or how to protect them, you should consult a competent intellectual property attorney. Additional information is available from the United States Patent and Trademark Office at www.uspto.gov.

 Patents

A patent for an invention is the grant of property rights to the owner or inventor, issued by the U.S. Patent and Trademark Office. The patent provides rights for up to 20 years for inventions divided into three categories: utility, design and plant patents. The patent grants "the right to exclude others from making, using, offering for sale, or selling" the invention in the United States or "importing" the invention into the United States.

<u>Utility Patents</u>

Utility patents protect processes, machines, articles of manufacture and compositions of matter. Examples are fiber optics, computer hardware, medications.

<u>Design Patents</u>

Design patents guard against the unauthorized use of new, original and ornamental design for articles of manufacture. The look of an athletic shoe, piece of sporting equipment or toy are examples of design patents.

<u>Plant Patents</u>

Plant patents are the way we protect invented or discovered asexually reproduced plant varieties. Hybrid tea roses, Silver Queen corn, Better Boy tomatoes are all types of plant patents.

 Trademarks

Trademarks are words, names, symbols or devices which are used in trade with goods to indicate the source of the goods and to distinguish them from the goods of others. Servicemarks are the same as trademarks except that they identify and distinguish the source of a service rather than a product. The term "trademark" and "mark" are commonly used to refer to both trademarks and servicemarks.

Trademark rights may be used to prevent others from using a similar mark or symbol, but not to prevent others from making the same goods or from selling the same goods and services under a different mark. Trademarks used in interstate or foreign commerce may be registed with the Patent and Trademark Office.

To protect your Trademark or claim rights in a mark, always use the "TM" or ® symbol. Trademarks that are registered with the Patent and Trademark Office may use the ® symbol. Proper use enhances a mark's ability to identify the origin of products or services, and minimizes the likelihood that a mark will become generic or unintentionally abandonded. Use the proper trademark notice ™ or ® and always use your trademark as an adjective. For example, calling a facial tissue a Kleenex® would be improper, as opposed to a Kleenex® facial tissue.

Trademarks, unlike patents, can be renewed forever as long as they are being used in business. The roar of the *MGM* lion, the pink of the *Owens-Corning* insulation, and the shape of a *Coca-Cola* bottle are familiar trademarks.

 Copyrights

Copyright is a form of protection provided to the authors of "original works of authorship" including literary, dramatic, musical, artistic and certain other intellectual works, both published and unpublished. The Copyright Act gives the owner of a copyright the exclusive right to reproduce the copyrighted work, to prepare derivative works, to distribute copies or phonorecords of the copyrighted work publicly, or to display the copyrighted work publicly.

Under the copyright law, the following seven types of works can be copyrighted:

- Literary works
- Musical works
- Dramatic works
- Pantomimes and Choreographic works
- Pictorial, Graphic and Sculptural works, including fabric designs
- Motion Pictures and other audio visual works
- Sound Recordings

The owner or creator has basic, common-law copyright protection automatically whenever an idea is put into a fixed form (writen in an article, recorded in a song, made into a videotape, or stored on a disk). Protection that's more likely to stand up in a legal fight can be obtained by placing the symbol © the year of first publication, and the name of the copyright holder prominently on every publication of the material. The protection is even stronger if a copyright application for artistic work is filed with the Federal Copyright Office.

The copyright protects the form of expression rather than the subject matter of the writing. For example, a description of a machine could be copyrighted, but this would only prevent others from copying the description; it would not prevent others from writing a description of their own or from making or using the machine.

The Library of Congress registers copyrights which last the life of the author plus 50 years. _Gone With The Wind_ (the book and the film), Beatles recordings, and video games are all works that are copyrighted.

Trade Secrets

A trade secret is different from a patent, trademark and copyright in that it is not formally protected under the law. A trade secret is a formula, process, design or compilation of information which is not generally known or reasonably ascertainable. By law, a trade secret has three parts: 1) the information, 2) the reasonable measures taken by the owner to keep it secret, and 3) the economic benefit from the trade secret being kept from being publicly known.

A company can protect its confidential information with nondisclosure contracts with its employees and partners. The protection of proprietary or confidential information allows for a perpetual monopoly in secret information. It does not expire, but the lack of formal protection means that a third party is not prevented from independently duplicating and using the secret information if it is discovered.

Systems Thinking

You've read the word 'system' in this book quite a few times and we're just getting started in our journey to quickly start a profitable business. I've been a follower of the ultimate systems guy and small business guru, Michael E. Gerber, for many years. In fact, I regularly teach the principles and encourage would-be entrepreneurs to read his most famous work, ***The E-Myth Revisited***, *Why Most Small Businesses Don't Work And What To Do About It.* If you ever hope to enjoy the lifestyle and financial success that likely drove you into this venture in the first place, you'll need to embrace this idea of systems thinking. The idea is something like this: Just because you are good at doing some activity, doesn't mean you can run a business that provides that activity. For example, just because you are really good at making homemade pies and cakes, doesn't mean you can run a bakery. That's the idea and story of *The E-Myth Revisited*. If you don't know Michael Gerber or have never read this book, I encourage you to do so. In fact, it's number one on my list of required reading for entrepreneurs.

Your goal is to graduate from being a:

Technician - someone who is good at doing a specific job or task, like an engineer, salesman or accountant,

to being a:

Manager - the one who manages the whole operation,

to finally becoming an:

Entrepreneur - one whose job it is to promote and position the business for growth and prosperity, but not the person who does the individual jobs or manages the people who do the jobs.

A technician can do a specific job or possesses a certain set of skills. Your job as a business owner is to identify the best way to perform the job and then document that system of performance so that any employee with the basic skill set for the job could step in and also perform the job at a consistent level. If you ever want to graduate from being the worker, you'll have to use your skills to create a system for doing the work that can be taught to others. In fact, you should approach your whole business from the point of view that you will franchise the business eventually. You likely will not actually franchise the business, but you should approach the management of your company with that perspective. With a franchise model, you can create a company that will run just as well when you are standing there as when you are not. This is really critical if you ever hope to be an owner and not an employee.

Think about your business in relation to one of the most famous franchises in the world; McDonald's. Everything at McDonald's is systemized. From how to prepare the store for opening in the morning to how to close it down at night, everything is documented and systemized. I was fortunate enough to work at McDonald's while I was in high school and college. I say fortunate, because not only did I have a job that provided needed funds to pay for my college education, but I also learned about business management from the experts in franchising. While you can't factor out every behavioral issue of employees, you can create a business that makes excellent profits that's based on a system that allows for incredibly high turnover of unskilled workers.

Hopefully, your business will not have 200 -300% turnover rates. But if it does, your systems will allow you to deal with that in a way that still ensures your business will operate in the same ways that it would if you were performing the jobs yourself.

Much of this systems thinking approach doesn't really take place until your business is up and running. However, as you design and organize your business for the first time, think about how you want to organize your operations and what is the best and most efficient way to perform the individual tasks. This is an excellent opportunity to get some of this work done. As you progress, you can continue to collect data and ideas for organizing and systemizing your processes when the time is right. One of the best ways to accomplish this systemizing process is through an operations manual.

Operations Manual

An operations manual will be your vehicle for documenting your business and systems. Just like at McDonald's, you'll need to refine the practices and procedures and document them in an operations manual. By defining the best practices in each area of the company, you'll ensure that subsequent employees will perform the duties and make the decisions involved in running your business the same way you would have them done. Your trainers will train new employees the same way each time and consistency will reign!

As you decide on the best way to do things, concentrate on your core business systems and constantly ask yourself how to design these systems so that they will support your customers. If you approach this entire process from the point of view of your customer, you'll have a better opportunity to eliminate barriers to providing excellent customer service. How will you use technology, people and processes to improve the customer's experience doing business with your company? If you can create systems and processes that make it easy and even pleasurable to do business with your company, you'll provide value to the customer relationship that they very rarely experience and almost never expect. Customers *always* want that kind of experience, but poorly run companies have conditioned them to expect less. A company that delivers that kind of easy and pleasurable experience will build a loyalty that is not defined by price.

One way to accomplish this documenting process is to create a table of contents for your operations manual. Once you have defined what will be included, set up a folder system for each topic heading. Some people like to use large envelopes to keep all the notes, lose paper, drawings, sketches, plans, copied documents and other work from getting lost during the creation process.

There are as many different ways of setting up and organizing your operations manual as there are different business operations. In general, you'll want to cover the major distinct operating areas of the business, the physical features of the business, and if appropriate, some introduction material relating to corporate history, philosophy, product and service offering and so forth. The exact contents will depend on the company operating philosophy, corporate culture and individual wishes of the owner.

The following outline represents a general purpose template to get you thinking about creating an operations manual for your business. Obviously, you'll want to add to and subtract from this template as appropriate.

Operations Manual Template - GENERAL

Introduction

Letter from President/Owner
Corporate Philosophy
Mission, Vision & Values
Company History & Timeline

Organization

Industry Overview
Description of Business
Product & Services Description
Critical Organization Contact Information
 Bank Information
 Corporate Attorney
 Corporate Address
 Public Relations Office
 Federal Employer Identification Number
 Certified Public Accounting Firm
Worker's Compensation Insurance Agent
 General Liability Insurance Agent
 Hazard Insurance Agent
Succession Plan

Emergency Procedures

In Case of Emergency Contacts
Robbery, Theft and Vandalism
Injury or Illness
Fire or Natural Disaster
Violent Customers
MSDS Policy & Information
Evacuation Procedures
Alarms, Locks and Keys
Municipal & Government Inspections

Operations Procedures

Business Opening Procedures
Business Closing Procedures
Security Systems & Measures
Housekeeping and Appearance Standards
Employee Scheduling
Duties and Checklists by Job
Theft & Loss Prevention
Transaction Procedures
>   Bank Deposits
>   Handling Cash & Cash Drawers
>   Credit Cards & Check Acceptance
>   Return Policy
>   NSF Check Return Policy
Daily Manager Reporting
Weekly & Monthly Sales & Goal Reporting

Manufacturing Procedures

Production Scheduling
Maintenance Operations
Stores & Supplies
Staffing
Material Handling
Shipping Operations
Loading Docks & Yard Operations
Safety
Machine Operations
Facility Operations & Maintenance
Production Reporting

Inventory Management & Merchandising

Approved Vendors
Inventory Controls
Min/Max Levels and Inventory Reordering
Warehouse Procedures
Product Pricing

Sales and Promotion Guidelines
Floor Plan & Displays

Human Resources

Job Descriptions & Expectations
Applications
Interviews, Selection & Hiring
EEO Policy
Compensation & Bonus Structure
Vacation Policy
Employee Benefits
Probationary Period
Performance Reviews
Harrassment & Discrimination Policy

Financial Management

Daily Reports
Monthly Reports
Month End Closing Procedures
Accounts Payable
Accounts Receivable Management
Financial Reporting Standards

Customer Service

Returns & Exchanges
Complaints
Special Product or Service Orders
General Product Knowledge
Sales Principles
Sales Associate Responsibilities to Customer
Sales Associate Authority for Complaint Resolution

Advertising & Marketing

Customer Analysis
Current Market Analysis
Budget

Goals & Objectives
Corporate Branding
Time Frames
Resource Needs
Monitor, Measure & Testing
Tactical Action Plans

See additional templates at **www.BusinessStart-up101.com.**

Part 3: Business Planning

"The market for something to believe in is infinite."

–Hugh MacLeod

Now that we've identified some of the mechanical issues associated with starting a business, it's time to turn our attention to our business model. That is, identifying our market, competition, customers and defining our product and service offering.

Market Research

In order to identify and understand your market, segments, competition, distribution channels and customers, you're going to have to do some research. Even a seasoned industry 'expert' will have to do some research when starting a new business. Where will you get the information that you need? There are many sources of information and in the age of the Internet, maybe in some cases, too much information. Be careful where your research produced information comes from. There are as many 'experts' as there are websites with content. Just because someone wrote a blog entry about your industry, doesn't mean the information is factual or that the blogger is an expert. Anyone can create a web site and pretend to be an expert. Some do this as a means of promoting a political position or they have a personal economic incentive. Keep in mind where your 'data' comes from and make sure it's a source that you trust.

Census Bureau – The Census Bureau has some excellent demographic information available from their website http://factfinder.census.gov/. This information is free to the public and is available from any computer with an internet connection. You can sort the information by state, county, city or even zip code level.

<u>Public Library</u> – The local public library has many sources of market data. Many larger libraries have extensive periodicals from multi-family apartment construction to zoo management. Look through the magazines and journals to see if they carry ones that might be interesting to your particular industry. They might have many years of old periodicals and newspapers. In addition, they will likely have technical and financial books relating to companies and industries that you can view in the reference section.

Many large libraries have a reference librarian whose job it is to help you find information that you need. If you are pleasant and courteous, they will normally bend over backwards to assist you in your search for information. If you explain that you are starting a company and trying to find some information about an industry, segment, or competitor, they will give you some possible sources and might even do some searching for you.

Library cards are available for free to members of the community. If you live out of town, you might have to pay a small fee for a library card, which gives you the privilege to check-out materials. However, for research purposes, you probably will not have to take anything home. You can do your research in the library and probably will not need an actual library card.

Virtual library cards are available for using the many sources of non-public information. These sources could be public policy institutes, research or databases maintained by universities, public or private companies, and other research related sites. The information is generally only available to educational or research organizations and requires a special subscription. Public libraries have these subscriptions and make them available to their patrons. This virtual library card can usually be used from your home computer by logging into the library's information portal.

Just ask the library employees if your local library offers a virtual library card.

University Library – Just like the public libraries, most university libraries are open for use by the local community. If you aren't sure, give them a call. For serious research about new or growing businesses, university librarians are generally happy to assist. They're used to working with students and will gladly help a small business person who approaches them with a friendly attitude and gracious spirit.

Trade Associations – Most industries have a trade association that serves as the advocate for the industry. In many large industries, there may be several different groups serving similar needs for different segments of the industry. You may have to join the association to get access to their data, but they typically are an excellent source of specific and relevant information about your industry. If you don't find what you're looking for on their web site, call the office and speak with a representative. Again, these individuals are generally more than willing to assist a potential new member find the information they are seeking.

Market Testing – If you need specific information about consumer buying habits, you probably need to do some market testing. The types of information you need might relate to how the shape and color of your product affects consumer behavior, or how your employee uniforms affects customer views on your professionalism. If your potential product roll-out is very large and costly, you will need some reliable consumer preference information. You can do this with focus groups, product testing, surveys and interviews among others. This type of research can be done by the owner, but unless you understand how this process works or have the time to research and study how to do it, it's better left to professionals. While this may be the most expensive type of market research you conduct, it may also be the most helpful.

You should conduct some market behavior research as a part of your everyday business information gathering. Test the response of your customers to different product colors, shapes and sizes. How does the way your employees are dressed affect customer behavior? What about how you greet your customers on the phone or in person? To be effective, you must measure what you're doing and the results you get. The only way to get valuable information is to make changes to your system and measure the results compared to the results you got before the change. Maybe you try several iterations before you hit on the best method or style. Data gathering in every part of your business is the only way to truly measure the variables in place and the results that were produced.

Defining the Market

Understanding your market is one of the important first steps in preparing to start a new business. Understanding how your market works, the size and potential for a new player in the existing market structure are key components. Who are your competitors and why would a potential customer buy from you? In many respects, understanding the market is the most important part of the start-up process.

While this part seems to be simple and is often overlooked or skipped, it requires a serious analysis of each component. Brainstorm and research each market segment in which you will compete, and then boil down the results into a form to help you 'see' the market at a glance. Once you've assembled all the information, list it in a matrix format to get an 'at a glance' view of your market. You may also use the Market Matrix Worksheet that is available for download at **www.BusinessStart-up101.com.**

- How big is the market?
- What are the different market segments?
- What market segment am I after? (Target Market)
- What % of the market share do I want?
- What % of the market share do I need?

Can the market support another competitor? Knowing how big the market is and who has the major share will help you determine your strategy. Based on your own financial projections, what share of the market do you represent? Is that reasonable? If the financial projections show you with a large percentage of the market share, do a reality check with your advisors to confirm your projections and assumptions.

If you are hoping to be a national market player, how will the large competitors in the market react to your entry into the market and subsequent rise from start-up to a real competitor?

Many markets likely already have a dominant player who serves a broad section of the market, perhaps operating across many different segments. How will you compete with this dominant player? Perhaps you can find a niche segment or sub-segment in which to operate. If you're not looking to awaken the sleeping giant, the major player in the market, perhaps your best bet is to think small. By that, I mean to operate within a small niche at first to prove your model and fine tune your business skills. After you have smoothed out the rough spots in your operating model, only then might you want to expand your business to serve a larger segment.

Distribution Channels

- What are the standard distribution channels for this industry?
- What is my distribution strategy?
- What channels will I use?
- How will we change your business model?
- Will you go directly to the market or use a partner?

How you go to market can be largely defined by your individual market. If everyone in the market uses the same distribution method, and your target customer prefers that method, then you're probably limited to operating largely with that distribution method. That's not to say you can't offer your products or services through other channels, but be prepared to be underwhelmed by the response from your customers. However, business is an ever changing dynamic, and new models are designed and tested every day. Who's to say your new distribution channel model isn't the next best method? Do your research, know your customer preferences and test your methods before investing lots of money in an untested method.

Defining The Market Worksheet

Define your market. How big is it? What are the distinct market segments?

Describe your market segment, its size and distribution channels.

Identifying the Competition

Competition

- Who are my competitors
    - What do they do well? (Strengths)
    - What do they do poorly? (Weaknesses)
    - What is their market share?
- What sets you apart from all the other competitors
- Direct Competitors
- Indirect Competitors

Direct competitors are those competitors who are in your same line of business offering substantially the same products and services that you plan to offer. If you have designed a new line of hand tools for the masonry trades, then your direct competitors are supply houses that serve these trades, the 'big box' DIY retail stores. But you may also have competition from other non-traditional competitors, indirect competitors, such as department stores that carry tools, like Sears, distributors like Harbor Freight and other online only distributors. While you don't want to spend too much time on the indirect competitors, don't forget they are out there and will have an influence on your customers.

You should conduct a strengths and weaknesses analysis on each of your major competitors. Do market research where necessary. You need to understand what it is that each of them does well and not so well.

Don't think for a moment that you don't have any competition. It's not true. You have competition. Even if there is a brand new market emerging, someone else can mobilize in reaction to it with more people and more money than you. This is reality check time. That you've poured your heart and soul and life savings into this venture is irrelevant. Your competition could care less. They are in the business to make money and you now represent a threat to them.

How will you differentiate yourself and your business from every other business in your market segment? This question is at the heart of your business model, your product or service offering and your distribution channel. How will you do business better, smarter, cheaper, faster or more responsive to customer needs than your competition? Be careful of going for the cheaper angle. Your biggest competitors probably have much better cost models than you and could easily destroy you in a price war. Customers don't always respond to the cheapest price model in the ways you would expect. You have to carefully consider your market segment, what your competition is doing, how they price and go to market and then find your niche in an under-served segment.

Pricing

- How does your competition price?
- How will you price?
- Why?
- What are the tradeoffs of pricing higher, lower, the same?
- How does market pricing relate to your costs?
- Why will your target market customers buy from you?

Can you make money in this business? How does your cost to produce the product or service relate to the prices your competition charges? What are the advantages and disadvantages of pricing higher or lower than your competition?

For a small business start-up, it is highly unlikely that you will be able to move the market to your costs. Unless you've discovered a way to make the product or service at significantly reduced costs, you should probably assume that you'll have to charge a price similar to your competition. If you think you can produce the product at a significantly reduced price, you should go back and confirm your numbers. Ask yourself, what's different about the way we will make the product and go to market that allows us to do it a reduced cost? Make sure you understand all the costs involved in going to market. Many large companies have whole teams of engineers and accountants studying cost reduction and best practices in manufacturing so that they can tweak another penny or nickel out of their costs. You don't have that kind of team and couldn't hope to buy in the quantities of your biggest competitors, except in rare circumstances.

Is it really an advantage to be the cheapest seller in the market? For many consumer products, Wal-Mart is the price leader. And with 2009 revenues of $401 Billion through 8,000 retail outlets, you'll never be able to compete with them on price. And do you really want to try? Having the lowest price may work against you depending on your market. If you are selling consumer products, then you'll need to be at least competitive with your pricing. But if you're selling high-tech scientific services, low prices may give your target customers the feeling that you aren't very good at what you do. The point is the price you charge for your products or services should be part of your strategy. Which market segments you serve, which customers you target, the specific product or service you offer, how you go to market and what prices you charge are all part of your model and should be thought about carefully with the end result of serving your target customers in mind. Don't pick any of those strategies haphazardly.

Defining the Competition Worksheet

Who are your direct competitors? What % of market share do they have?

Who are your indirect competitors?

Identifying Your Customers

- Who are my customers?
  - Type
    - Business-to-Business
    - Individuals
    - Both
  - Demographics
    - Age
    - Sex
    - Marital Status
    - Income
    - Education
  - Location
    - Where do they live?
    - Where do they work?
    - Where do they play?
    - On what routes do they drive?
  - Behavior
    - What makes them a target customer?
    - What about their behavior makes them interesting to me?
    - What makes my product interesting to them?

We find that many times small businesses don't really understand their customer. What about their income, age or behavior makes them interesting to you? What about your product, service, mission or corporate philosophy makes you interesting to your potential customer?

Be very cautious about blindly buying-in to social behavioral 'norms'. Don't assume that because your target customer is environmentally conscious, that he will pay more for your 'green' product or service. Consumers are usually motivated by price and personal convenience more so than social activism. So don't drink your own Kool-Aid.

Clearly define your target customer in the four categories listed above. Depending on your business, you may have defined an even more precise measurement system. If you have actual historical data from this or another business that closely matches yours, use that information to get a better feel of your customer and their behaviors.

Defining the Customer Worksheet - INDIVIDUALS

Using the categories below, define to the best of your knowledge, your primary customers.

Type: ___ Business-to-Business
       ___ Individuals
       ___ Both

Demographics: Clearly define the major customer category by demographics.

Age: _____ - _____

Sex: _____ Male _____ Female _____ Both

Marital Status: ____ Married ____ Single ____Divorced

Income: $_____ to $_____

Education: ____ HS ____ College ____ Advanced Degree

Location: Are there specific locations where they

Live? _____

Work? _____

Play? _____

Driving Routes? _____

_____

Behavior: Is there something about their behavior that makes them interesting?

Hobbies? _____

_____

Interests? _____

_____

Political/Religious Beliefs? _____

_____

Buying Habits? _____

_____

School/Sports Supporter? _____

_____

Other: _____

_____

_____

_____

_____

_____

Defining the Customer Worksheet - BUSINESSES

Using the categories below, define to the best of your knowledge, your primary customers.

Delivery Channel: ____ Business-to-Business
   ____ Wholesale/Distributor
   ____ Manufacturer's Rep
   ____ Retail

Demographics: Clearly define the major customer category by demographics.

Size: $_____ Assets $_____ Sales

Location: _____ Local _____ Regional _____ National

# of Employees: _____ to _____

Type: _____ Retail
   _____ Wholesale
   _____ Manufacturing
   _____ Service

Presence: _____ Brick & Mortar
   _____ Virtual
   _____ Stand Alone
   _____ Strip Complex
   _____ Industrial Park

Behavior: How do they operate and make buying decisions?

Buying Decision: _____ Local _____ Centralized

Function: _____ Purchasing Department
                   _____ Store Manager
                   _____ Manufacturing Department
                   _____ Other: _____

Other Characteristics:

_____

_____

_____

_____

_____

_____

_____

_____

S.W.O.T. Analysis

At this point in the process you should have a good idea of the trends in your industry and within your specific market segment; what your competitors do well and not-so-well, and what your customers need, want and desire. It's time to put all this information together in the form of a SWOT Analysis. SWOT stands for **S**trengths, **W**eaknesses, **O**pportunities and **T**hreats. The SWOT Analysis is at the heart of the strategic planning process.

Management theory typically breaks down the SWOT into internal and external environment, where strengths and weaknesses are internal to the firm and opportunities and threats are external to the market factors. While this breakdown makes sense in many instances, it can sometimes be confusing. (Are the strengths and weaknesses of your competitors Opportunities or Threats?) What is important to understand is that the SWOT analysis of your firm will identify your resources and capabilities and how they match up against the other players in your market. It will identify what your firm is prepared to do better than your competition and what your customers expect that your operation is ill prepared to provide.

 Strengths

What are your organizations strengths?

Your strengths should be measured relative to your competition and the expectations of your customers. Following this internal-external theme, strengths are an internal analysis of how your company is prepared to compete in the market. Some examples of strengths are:

- Patents
- Proprietary systems
- Production cost advantages
- Technology advantages
- Financial reserves
- Locational or geographic advantages
- Experienced staff
- Strong brand awareness
- Certifications or accreditations

Stengths can come in many different forms, whether people, technology, brand, financial resources or even strong customer loyalty.

 Weaknesses

What are your organizations weaknesses?

Like strengths, your weaknesses should be measured relative to your competition and customer expectations. In some cases, a weakness is the flip-side of a strength. While experienced staff may be a strength in providing customer support, it's also expensive to have a large and experienced staff. Also, having plenty of production capacity may be a strength, but it's also a weakness in that your machines aren't running constantly throughout the day. Like strengths, the weaknesses analysis is a look inside your organization and how it's prepared to compete in the marketplace. Some examples of weaknesses are:

- No patent protection
- Weak brand awareness
- Poor or no reputation in market
- Weak financial position
- Low employee morale
- Poor distribution networks
- Lack of technological infrastructure
- Weak management team

It's important to make an honest assessment of your position within the market.

Opportunities

What are your organization's opportunities?

With the opportunities analysis, we get to look outside the company at the market environment. How is your competition responding to the customer's needs? What niches are left unfilled or what product lines unproduced or poorly serviced? Examples of opportunities are:

- Regulatory opportunities
- Competitor exit from market
- New vertical market development
- New technology opportunity
- Major contract appropriation
- Seasonal product demand
- International trade barrier removal
- Tax code change
- Material processing improvement
- Major population shift

Threats

What are your organization's threats?

Like opportunities, threats come from the market, or external environment. Examples of threats are:

- Political/Legislative changes
- Technology changes
- International trade barriers
- Substitute products
- Change in consumer tastes
- National economic weakness

Changes to the external environment may provide opportunities to some and present threats to others. Depending on your own strengths and weaknesses, your company may view these market changes differently than does your competition.

S.W.O.T. Analysis Worksheet

Complete a S.W.O.T. Analysis on your company.

Strengths (Internal):

Weaknesses (Internal):

Opportunities (External):

Threats (External):

Product & Service Plan

Describe, in detail, the products and services you will be selling. Your description should include a general description of each product or service, plus pricing models and distribution channels for each product or service.

You have just completed a S.W.O.T. Analysis, and should have in mind the opportunities and threats in the market. Your company strengths and weaknesses will help you evaluate which opportunities are right for you and the threats to avoid. As you develop your products and service offering, keep in mind the needs, wants and desires of your target customer. You might think that the latest add-on or upgrade to a do-dad is the hottest next thing in the market, but does your customer? Many a product or service has been designed and marketed only to find that no real market exists. While the company owner spent lots of money developing marketing plans and buying advertising, if there is no real market for a product or service, that money will have been wasted.

Talk to your customers, conduct focus groups or other market studies. Make sure that your prospective customers actually want to pay money for your particular product or service. One way is to select some individuals who are in your target customer group and ask them. If the difference in color, shape, size and packaging is potentially important to the marketing effort, take the necessary time to understand these factors. If your plan is big and the risk is high, you might need to hire a market research firm to help determine which characteristics will be included in your product or service.

Make sure you understand the difference between features and benefits. A feature is a factual statement about a product or service; it's what products have. A benefit is what those features

mean; it describes why your customer should care. Theodore
Levitt, a 19th Century economist and Harvard University professor
described the difference like this: "People don't want to buy
a quarter-inch drill, they want a quarter-inch hole."

Your customers only care about benefits. They are *what's in it for
me* kind of people. In fact, everyone is a *what's in it for me* kind of
person. As a manufacturer, you care about your product features;
it has a little handle here, this one is blue, that button makes it fly
higher, those straps keep it from falling off. As consumers, your
customers only care about your product benefits; it's easy to carry,
it matches my carpet, I can feel the exilarition, it's safe. Just keep
in mind that only you and your salespeople care about features.
Your customers only care about benefits.

Marketing Plan

You've done all your research and think you're ready to open up
shop and start selling your product. How do you know you've
got the product or service right? Like every other step in this
process, you need a well defined goal and plan to get you there.
While most new entrepreneurs think developing the financial
statements is the hardest part of the process, it's the marketing
plan that probably is least understood. Outside of running out of
cash, lacking a marketing plan is one of the leading causes of
business failure. Having the right product, at the right price, in
the right place, with the right promotion, is a balancing act that is
way more difficult than putting together a simple mathematical
model based on addition and subtraction.

A marketing plan is a three-part model that consists of 1) an
analysis of current market conditions, 2) a strategy for defining
overall plans, budgets and timetables and 3) implementation
tactics or action plan to make it all happen.

Market Situation Analysis

This first part of the marketing plan requires us to take a look back at the industry. What are the current conditions taking place in the market? What are the trends in the segment where we will operate and what are the strengths and weaknesses of our competitors, both direct and indirect? Next, review your target customer. Identify their location and anything about their demographic that would affect how they make buying decisions, in addition to their needs, wants and desires.

<u>Unique Value Proposition</u>

What makes your company so special? If *you* don't know, how will your customers know? Hopefully, you have a very clear and organized way of thinking about how you are different from your competition. We call this your unique value proposition (UVP) or unique selling poposition (USP).

You probably decided to go into your particular line of business because you have a clearly defined UVP. You hate the way your industry or old employer handles a particular situation and you want to open a company that does it differently. Maybe it has to do with building customer loyalty or how you treat employees. Whatever your particular UVP, you need to define it in a way that your customers can not only understand it, but also embrace it.

Let's face it; your customers do not care that you feel passionately about a particular cause or situation. They only care about what it means to them. If you feel strongly that you will use only recycled packaging and shipping materials, what does that mean for them? If you haven't got a good answer to that, then you need to put your thinking cap on and figure it out. It's not unlike the discussion about features and benefits. Don't let your passion become a feature to your customers. If you can't put into words how you are different and why your customers will care, then they probably will not care, and you probably are not different from your competition. Be honest with yourself, and don't try to fabricate something out of nothing.

Brand

What's your brand? We used to think of BRAND as a logo or group of stylized words and colors. Clever marketeers even dream up fanciful words like *ultra-surfactant quotient* and  X-43 *Super Clean* to push their brands. As far back as the 1960s Sears used the toughskins *tri-blend* fabric as a means to identify their brand of jeans as better and more durable than the other brands on the market. With the advent of the infomercial, secret code words have abounded. But in the infomercial world, do savvy consumers and businesses really fall for the code word or slick logo as a replacement for the values of the company?

Your brand should be an extention of who your company is, what it stands for and how it does business. If that sounds like a tall order, it is. Creating the perfect marketing package takes more than just combining your products with cool logos to create a brand. And branding is way more than just fancy marketing. While the slick marketing piece will help play a role, it's the marriage of your brand message with the actions of the company that ultimately matter. In other words, reality must match your branding.

You have to first understand that all businesses are really providing a service. Whether your company is a 'service' business or a manufacturer, distributor, retail or wholesale, you are really providing a service. And what's worse, today's on-line virtual world has turned every competitor in the world into *your* competitor. The only real distinction comes down to service. It's not what you sell, it's how you sell it and how you support your customers after the purchase. How does your brand tell that story and does the brand story match the reality?

<u>Product or Service</u>

What is your product or service? You should be able to define your product in terms of what it does for the customer. How does it make the customer's life better, easier, faster or cheaper? How will your customer's life be improved by buying your product? What makes your product superior over every other similar product already on the market? If you can't think of a good answer to these questions, your customer probably can't either.

Many producers see their product as the final result of their work instead of the beginning of the process. What you're looking for is a solution to your customer's needs. You must constantly evaluate what you make, how you sell it, how the product is actually used from the perspective of your customer. You must look at your whole business model from the eyes of your customer. If they really like your product better than your competition, but navigating your ordering system is too complicated, you'll lose the sale. If your product is priced perfectly to generate new business, but you have customer service employees with a bad attitude, what difference does any of your work make? When you think of product, you should really think process. You not only must have a great product, priced competitively, but you also must have systems and procedures that make doing business with your company easy and enjoyable.

Mission Statement

A mission statement is a simple statement of what business you are in and why. This statement is the responsibility of the owners

and senior management of a company to define and implement.
Once written, the mission statement serves as the ground rules for
operating the business. That is, each major decision of the
company should somehow support the mission, vision or values
of the organization. Small business owners ask if the mission
statement isn't just some big company nonsense made up by
Fortune 500 executives without a real job. I think the mission
statement is just as important for small companies, maybe more
important, than for their multi-national counterparts. You should
be able to use your mission statement to guide the company as
you grow. If you are considering new ventures or product lines,
they should first be measured against your mission statement to
see if they support the overall goals of the organization. If not,
you should reconsider the venture or your mission. All activities
of your company should further your mission.

How can you succeed in a small business if you don't know what
business you are in and why you are in that business? Without a
clearly defined statement that you support and believe, you may
wander aimlessly among your competitors trying different
courses and taking different paths without any real goal.
Especially for a small business, your mission statement should be
a defining document of your beliefs and objectives for going into
business in the first place.

A mission statement can be a simple sentence or declaration, or a
more complete summary of an organization's beliefs, values and
vision for its future. If you have a strong drive and vision for your
company, here is your chance to share that belief and value
system with your employees and customers.

Your mission statement may include any of the following
categories. But for it to be effective in guiding your company

direction and operations, it should be a clearly stated and honestly held declaration of your beliefs, not some phony corporatespeak.

 Mission – Your mission is a basic statement describing the overall purpose of your company. It is the first strategic decision the company should take. The mission should define your direction, priorities and what sets you apart from your competitors. It should reflect the personality of the owners and help build the image of the organization. Ideally, it will motivate your employees and clarify the direction you will take on your path to success.

Vision – Your vision statement includes a clear description of the company and its operations. It should paint a picture of an ideal future. The vision statement declares what we want to be.

Values – The values statement reflects the core ideology of your organization, those deeply held values that do not change with strategies and managers. Your company should live and breathe its value statement and be reflected in how you carry out your mission.

Perhaps the best way to define the mission, vision and values, is to give a good example.   The following is the mission statement of the Coca-Cola Company headquartered in Atlanta, Georgia:

Our Mission
Our Roadmap starts with our mission, which is enduring. It declares our purpose as a company and serves as the standard against which we weigh our actions and decisions.

To refresh the world...
To inspire moments of optimism and happiness...
To create value and make a difference.

Our Vision
Our vision serves as the framework for our Roadmap and
guides every aspect of our business by describing what we
need to accomplish in order to continue achieving
sustainable, quality growth.

People: Be a great place to work where people are inspired
to be the best they can be.

Portfolio: Bring to the world a portfolio of quality
beverage brands that anticipate and satisfy people's desires
and needs.

Partners: Nurture a winning network of customers and
suppliers, together we create mutual, enduring value.

Planet: Be a responsible citizen that makes a difference by
helping build and support sustainable communities.

Profit: Maximize long-term return to shareowners while
being mindful of our overall responsibilities.

Productivity: Be a highly effective, lean and fast-moving
organization.

Live Our Values
Our values serve as a compass for our actions and describe
how we behave in the world.

Leadership: The courage to shape a better future
Collaboration: Leverage collective genius
Integrity: Be real
Accountability: If it is to be, it's up to me
Passion: Committed in heart and mind
Diversity: As inclusive as our brands
Quality: What we do, we do well

This mission statement is rather long and complex. It identifies a
strategy and passion for the company products and how it will
interact with its customers and investors. A mission statement

need not be several pages long. This example from Briston-Myers Squib, headquartered in New York City, is an excellent example of getting straight to the point:

> To discover, develop and deliver innovative medicines that help patients prevail over serious diseases.

Whether your mission statement is long and involved or short and sweet, it must be real. You customers and employees will be turned off by marketing hype that doesn't reflect the way you behave.

Defining Your Mission Statement Worksheet

What is your company mission?

Define your company vision:

Define your company values:

Marketing Strategy

Developing a marketing strategy is a key element in business success. Your business will require some level of marketing. Whether you use your own word of mouth or a national television advertising campaign, you'll need to find a way to tell people and businesses about your product. Marketing plans don't have to be complicated, but they do need to be well thought out. Your marketing plan should include at least the following:

Identify the Goals

What do you want the marketing plan to accomplish? How long will it take? You need to establish specific market objectives and timeframes for accomplishing your goals. If you haven't identified specifics, at best you'll spin your wheels and not accomplish much and at worst, waste a pile of money and get nothing out of it.

Identify the Message

What's the message you want your customers to associate with your business name or product? Keep it simple, descriptive of some benefit to your customer or problem solved, and differentiate your company from your competitors. Do you have a secret weapon? Do you have a product or service that nobody else has? If you do, great, use it to your advantage. If not, you need to keep your message focused on your customer, fulfilling their needs and solving their problems.

Identify the Budget

How much will you spend? Don't start asking that question when you get the bill from the advertising sales rep. Define the budget for marketing your product up front when developing the plan and then manage to it.

How Will You Measure

How will you measure and how will you define success? It's important to identify these issues before you begin. If you don't know what the end result should look like, how will you know if you got there or not? And, if you don't get what you hoped for, how will you change your plan to better achieve your goals?

You will need a way to test your results so that you can make improvements to the plan. If you're looking at a radio spot to promote a particular product or service, maybe you run two different spots to determine which wording and portrayal works best. Maybe two different print ads could be used to see which draws more calls from interested customers. Make sure to include a different website, phone number, email or identifier so that you can tell which ad drove which result. Some people will remember a radio spot from several years ago or confuse your business with a competitor's ad.

You must constantly monitor, measure and test your promotional programs for effectiveness. If they aren't working, figure out why and make the necessary changes. Don't launch a promotional campaign and then forget about it. The ad sales people love customers who do that. They can sell you spots without ever having to answer for the promotional effectiveness. That's the same as a big tattoo on your forehead that says "SUCKER."

How Will You Price

What will you charge for your product? Why? Will you have different pricing models for a retail environment vs. a wholesale environment? How does your price compare to that of your competitors? How does your price compare to your cost of production? What are the benefits of being cheaper than your competitors? Are there benefits to being more expensive? How will you use payment terms and customer accounts to support your sales and financial goals?

Don't forget to think about total cost of product ownership. If the cost of your product doesn't end with the initial purchase, your customer will certainly be considering the total cost of ownership. If your sales price is cheap but operating the product is very expensive, your customer could become dissatisfied. Think about how your price compares to the cost of owning your product.

Where Will You Sell

Where will you sell your product? How will you go to market? Will you sell directly to the public through a retail environment, on-line to wholesalers, or something else? Will this be a catalog or direct mail type environment?

By this point in the evaluation and research process, you've probably already determined the selling location, whether by industry convention, competitor practices, or the great deal your brother-in-law gave you on a lease. Do a reality check with your advisors at this point. Discuss how the product, price and place solve problems for your customers and whether you're giving them what they want.

Implementation

The implementation stage is the action plan for putting your strategy into practice. The implementation phase of your plan could have dozens of different tactics for promoting and advertising your products or company. The specific tactics you choose will depend on your specific situation, budget, goals and timeframe. We'll cover some of the more common ways to promote your products. This is only a small list of possible implementation tactics. For an indepth guide on marketing tactics, review Jay Conrad Levinson's bestseller *Guerilla Marketing*: *Easy and Inexpensive Strategies for Making Big Profits from Your Small Business*. Of course, this is on our recommended reading list.

<u>Website</u>

Every business needs a website, period. If you have no intentions of using your site for the recruitment of customers, then you need it for general reference. In today's business environment, a business without a website is not viewed as a serious business. Even if your site is only serving as a business card with contact information and hours of operation, it's often the first impression you give to potential customers. Websites are easy to create and cheap. There's really no excuse for not having some kind of web presence.

<u>Marketing Collateral</u>

From business cards to brochures, product data sheets to samples, marketing collateral should define your brand and your products. Most small business owners can't afford fancy, Fifth Avenue created marketing material. Consider how you can stretch your budget to get the best material available. Even if you don't have much of a budget, don't put out crummy material. Some items can be printed or even copied in black and white on a copier. A product data sheet or Material Safety Data Sheet (MSDS) probably doesn't need to be a four-color print job. If you have to choose between good design and good color/materials/printing, choose good design. A well designed marketing piece can be used for many years. As your buget increases, you can change the printing or medium to spruce up the piece. However, a cheap design will look cheap no matter how fancy the printing or paper.

If you can only afford to produce one good piece of marketing collateral, make it your business card. You'll hand out your business card several hundred times a year. In many cases, your business card will be the only piece of collateral that a prospective customer will see. Spend the extra money to get your card designed by a professional so that you can always put your best foot forward with every contact.

Advertising

Advertising for your small business can take many different forms; from television or radio spots to sponsoring the high school yearbook. Advertising can easily become a black hole where money goes and never returns. This is one area where having a well defined budget and expectations are important. Know up front how much you can spend in advertising and how you will measure your success. If your first attempt doesn't work, change your approach or change your form. Many advertising options for small business fall under the category of 'donations' rather than advertising. Don't expect a high school yearbook ad to create new sales leads for you. However, advertising in a sports or arts program may lead to new customers. Which form of advertising you use will depend on your customer base and product line. It's usually a good idea to take small steps so that you can measure your success before spending big bucks on a full-blown campaign.

Direct Marketing

Direct marketing can include such approaches as direct mail, email, phone solicitation and lead generation. If you are using purchased mailing or calling lists, it's important to first define the type of lead for which you are looking. Most list agencies will be able to sort out their database into subgroups that meet your criteria. If you're selling industrial supplies and equipment, it doesn't do any good to solicit families. If you're selling cosmetics, you're probably wasting your time soliciting sporting venues. The more clearly you can define your customer, the better your list agency will be able to define the list you purchase.

If you plan to use phone solicitation, be careful. The industry has suffered at the hands of most companies who abuse the method. The national do not call lists may also make the available names less valuable. This approach is best left to large companies who really know how to use it.

Depending on your business and market, direct mail may be an excellent choice for contacting customers and generating leads. This is where getting a good list is really important. Define your customer and purchase a list that is as close to it as possible.

Networking

Networking is a free or low-cost promotion strategy that puts you in front of customers, competitors, other local business owners and employees and individuals who can help promote your business by word of mouth. While there are many organized networking events through business groups or civic clubs, it can also take place in a casual and opportunistic way.

If you are a member of local business groups such as the chamber of commerce or a BNI group, don't attempt to meet as many people as possible and hand out all your business cards. The idea with networking is to make deep connections with a few selected individuals' and bring value to the relationship. That is, find out about the other individuals business and find ways to make connections, introductions or referrals for them.

Don't try to make a sale in the first five minutes of talking. In fact, don't try to make a sale at all. Successful networking is about giving, not getting. If you give on your side of the relationship, the other side will do the same. You will build a valuable business relationship and over time have a network of people promoting your business for you.

Networking is a long-term process. It will not always generate immediate results. While you may get lucky, plan on developing a network of business partners and friends who support each other, direct leads to each other, and serve as resources to support each other's business.

Public Relations

While *public relations* has a different meaning in a large corporate setting, the small business can use many free methods to get their word out. It is in this context that I refer to public relations for small business. Some examples are:

- Press Releasees
- Website Blogs
- Social Networking
- Be Newsworthy
- Become an Expert
- Guerilla Marketing Tactics

One of best tools in the small business owner's public relations tool box is the press release. A well written press release is bound to get some mention in the local business section of the newspaper. In the best possible scenario, this might lead to an article or television interview. News outlets are constantly looking for interesting news and public interest stories. While they have lots of national and state stories they can carry, they'd much rather tell a local story. You just need to give them a compelling reason to do so.

When writing a press release, follow the standard industry format. If you don't know how to write a press release, then do a little research so that you can utilize the proper format and tell a newsworthy story. If your press release is seen as an advertisment, it likely won't get mentioned. The local media wants to help; you just have to do your part.

Social Networking

Social networking has become a popular promotional tactic only in the past couple of years. It's based on the premise that by building personal relationships with people, they will be more likely to buy your products when they need them or recommend your company to a friend who is in need of products like you sell. It can be a bit of a challenge to justify this activity in terms of time and costs, because it seems to be a large black hole where you pour your time. The costs associated with the social networking activities are low in terms of hard dollars spent. It's really a question of your time.

There are dozens of different social networking sites and different brands pop up every day. As of the writing of this book, the following social networking sites were fairly effective for mainstream work.

Twitter - microblogging site that enables users to send 'tweets', messages of 140 characters or less. It's an excellent tool for communicating with customers and presenting your brand. The search engines aparently give tweets favorable recognition and heavy keyword use can bring traffic to your site.

Facebook - is a social networking site where users can add and communicate with friends, send messages and build an elaborate profile complete with pictures, video and games. Facebook has recently added the ability to create business pages, an area which is growing rapidly. The complete extent of the benefit is yet unknown as this media is in the infancy stage. I expect it will continue to grow and become one of the most favored venues for businesses, even more important than a company web page in the future.

Facebook is excellent for engaging people who like your company or for promoting your brand. It's unlikely to generate massive amounts of unique traffic to your site in a viral way like Twitter can, but a steady network of friends can be built. There appears to be little value for search engine optimization from Facebook.

When we discuss search engine optimization, we're talking about Google. And since Google doesn't disclose how it ranks sites, this is a fairly hypothetical discussion based on clues from experts in this area. Outside of Google's analytical group, nobody really knows for sure how this works.

LinkedIn - is a social networking site for business professionals. It's essentially an elaborate professional resume. The service is an excellent means of branding for a professional, but it does less than most other sites at communicating to a particular group and generating traffic.

YouTube - is a video sharing website where users can upload and share videos. YouTube has seen phenomenal growth in recent years and is one of the best social networking sites for corporate branding, communication with customers and promoting your corporate website.

Digg – is a social news site where users can discover and share news content. While the site's few weaknesses are in the area of corporate communication, it does an excellent job of creating brand recognition, generating traffic and creating links that promote your website. Press releases and objective press will garner favorable coverage and have the potential for huge traffic spikes to your website.

StumbleUpon - is a social news community where members can discover and share webpages. While its weaknesses are direct customer communication and brand exposure, it does a good job of generating traffic to your website and generating search engine ratings.

Please recognize that by the time I finish typing this page, the social media players will have changed. These are just a few of the more important players in the social media market as of mid-2010. This is a fast moving medium and one that takes a considerable time investment. However, the payoff is huge traffic, brand awareness and customer communication. In 2010, most marketing experts think that social media is currently the next best thing since the bread slicer.

The Elevator Pitch

'So, what do you do?' How do you answer this question? It's called the elevator pitch and it may be the most important 10 - 30 seconds of your business life. Whether at a cocktail party, convention, business meeting or chance meeting, you are frequently asked what you do and have only a short window to engage your target with a compelling and interesting response that will make them ask more questions about your business.

An elevator pitch is a *brief* statement about who you are, what your business does and why anyone should care. The emphasis should be on why anyone should care. Here's the idea: you're in an elevator with a potential business investor or customer and they ask what you do. You have about 30 seconds, or the length of the elevator ride to tell them about your business and get them intrigued enough to keep talking to you when you reach the lobby.

Write out your elevator pitch and practice saying it in a relaxed and confident tone. Only you know your business and the different aspects of your work. You will need different elevator pitches for different situations and audiences. The only way to get good at this is to script the pitch and practice delivering it. Often you'll find that in saying out loud what you have written, it doesn't really work. Don't just read your script in your mind, say it out loud and practice in front of people who can give you constructive criticism.

What should you include in your elevator pitch? Here are a few thoughts to help you craft your ideal message:

How are you unique? – Why is your business or service any different than your competitors?

Speak to your customer's pain - Nobody cares that you have a speciality food shop. But if you have a food store that specializes in fully prepared meals ready to eat for working parents with families, now that might be really helpful and convenient for working parents.

Make it intersesting – An excellent elevator pitch should get you pumped up. If you're flat and lifeless, why would your prospect care what you're saying? If you have a great story or passion, work that into your pitch.

Keep it simple – You can't make a single story work for every situation and every prospect. You need to build an arsenal of components that you know backwards and forwards that can be woven together for just the right message for each audience. Write down each message variation and re-write them until they are perfect. Then, practice, practice, practice.

It's not about you – In case you missed that point already, it's about your customers and how you can make their life better. Your customers don't care about you. They only care about themselves. If you can keep that point in mind, you'll have a better chance of developing an interesting elevator pitch. Remember: **THEM** – not you.

Elevator Pitch Worksheet

Using the components below to craft your elevator pitch.

How are you unique?

Define your customer's pain:

How will your company fix their pain?

Elevator Pitch First Drafts

List three or more markets or customers then target your elevator pitch towards them.

Market 1: _____

Market 2: _____

Market 3: _____

Part 4: Business Financials

"No idea is so good it can't be improved."

–Tom Kelley

Now that we've identified our markets and customers, and clearly defined our product or service, it's time to look at the financial viability of our model. We'll begin by looking at start-up costs, then learn some tools for analyzing our business model.

Bootstrapping Your Business

When analyzing the expenses you will encounter, the equipment you will need and the location from which you will operate, it's good to do a reality check. What alternatives are available to buying this item? We like to use the *Buy – Lease – Rent – Borrow* analysis. When evaluating alternatives, ask if, rather than buying an item, you can lease it, rent it, or borrow someone else's? The advantages and costs of each approach break down as follows:

<u>*Buy*</u> – requires the highest cash up front, but you then own the item forever. However, if you have to borrow money to finance the purchase, you've created a long-term financial arrangement that makes disposal of an asset more difficult. The cost of money involved in the financing also increases the cost of owning the asset.

<u>Lease</u> – requires less cash up front than buying, but requires a long-term financial commitment that makes it difficult to return the item before the contract ends.

<u>Rent</u> – requires less cash up front like the lease, and generally has a short-term or month-to-month or even shorter financial commitment. Generally, this method allows you to pay for the item's use for the specific period in which you'll actually use it. The cost to use the asset per use denomination (hour, day,

pounds, etc.) is higher than buying or leasing, but you only pay for the time you have the equipment. This is an excellent choice for start-ups, especially if you don't need the item every day or every week.

Borrow – this 'financing method' involves back scratching and barter. Can you lend something to another business owner in exchange for borrowing something from him? I'm aware of a business man with artistic capabilities who traded some landscape paintings for orthodontic care. While this is a personal example, it's the perfect illustration of the concept.

Maybe you know someone with large real estate holdings with a vacant property you can use for a few months until you get up and running. Maybe your father-in-law will allow you to use his tractor with a forklift attachment over the winter to help out before you lease or buy a forklift.

These are four alternatives for acquiring assets for your new business. I'm sure you can think of others. Keep these in mind as you go through the following sections to determine your start-up costs. Maybe you can apply this same strategy to other types of expenses.

Start-up Costs Worksheets

These start-up cost worksheets have been broken down into 5 categories:

1. Business Formation Expenses
2. Business Location Expenses
3. Manufacturing & Distribution Expenses
4. Office Equipment Expenses
5. Other Business Expenses

This is not meant to be a complete list of all possible expenses, but rather a good starting point. Many of these expenses will not apply to your business or industry. Some expenses are one-time and others are on-going. Use these lists to help you brainstorm all the potential expenses associated with starting your business.

Discuss occupancy costs with prospective landlords, business formation costs with your attorney or CPA. These individuals should be able to give you historical expense levels for your industry or general business expenses like those associated with leasing your building such as common area maintenance (CAM), insurance and snow removal expenses. City officials, insurance agents and utility departments can help with the other expense estimates.

Business Formation Expense

Item	Estimate
Legal Consultation Fees	$
Corporate Legal Document Preparation	$
Local/County/State Filing Fees	$
State Initial Business Privilege Tax	$
Local Business Licenses	$
Tax/CPA Consultation Fees	$
Trademark & Service Mark Fees	$
Copyright & Patent Registration Fees	$
Insurance Expenses	$
Owners & Directors Errors & Omissions	$
Owner Life Insurance	$
Product Liability Coverage	$
Employee Health Insurance & Other Benefits	$
Worker's Compensation Insurance	$
Bank Fees	$
Account Opening Fees	$
Printed Check Fees	$
Other Banking Services Fees	$
Other:	$
Other:	$
Other:	$
Other:	$
Other:	$
Total Business Formation Expense	**$**

Business Location

Item	Estimate
Building Occupancy Charges	$
Building Rent or Lease	$
Annual/Quarterly CAM Charges	$
Building Leasehold Improvements	$
Real Estate Taxes	$
Special School or Other Taxes	$
Snow Removal Assessments	$
Fire Dept. Inspection	$
Sprinkler System Inspection & Certification	$
Insurance Expenses	$
Building & Contents Hazard Insurance	$
General Business Liability Insurance	$
Leased Equipment Coverage	$
Other Insurance:	$
Other Insurance:	$
Utility Deposits	$
Electricity	$
Natural Gas	$
Heating Oil	$
Water	$
Sewer	$
Utility Co-Op Fees	$
Telephone	$
Trash & Rubbish Services	$
Signage Expenses	$
Building Signs	$
Truck/Vehicle Signs	$
Advertising Signs	$
Other:	$
Other:	$
Total Business Location Expense	**$**

Manufacturing/Distribution Equipment Expense

Item	Estimate
Delivery Truck	$
Manufacturing & Fabrication Equipment	$
Manufacturing Machines	$
Manufacturing Consumables	$
Manufacturing Storage	$
Product Station-to-Station Transportation	$
Tools	$
Warehouse Equipment	$
Forklift, Pallet Jacks & Hand Trucks	$
Dock Plates & Wheel Chocks	$
Warehouse Racks & Ladders	$
Fencing & Product Security	$
Conveyor Systems	$
RFID or SKU Identification System	$
Warehouse Security System	$
Maintenance Supplies	$
Hand Tools	$
Warehouse Supplies	$
Hardhats	$
Ear, Eye & Hand Protection	$
Back Support Belts	$
First Aid Kit & Supplies	$
Fire Extinguishers	$
Box Cutters	$
Hand Tools	$
Rope, Twine & Product Containment Supplies	$
Carton & Corrugated Bailer	$
Paper Supplies	$
Shipping Supplies	$
Boxes, Cartons & Envelopes	$

Carton Tape	$
Strapping System & Supplies	$
Package Labels	$
Package Scale	$
Other:	$
Other:	$
Other:	$
Total Manufacturing/Distribution Expense	**$**

Office Equipment & Supplies Expenses

Item	Estimate
Office Furniture	$
Desks, Desk Chairs & Guest Chairs	$
File Cabinets & Book Cases	$
Cubicle Partitions	$
Copy & Fax Machine	$
Adding Machines & Calculators	$
Time Clock or Time System	$
Shredder or Secure Recycling System	$
Telephone System & Desk Phones	$
Cell Phones & Service	$
Computers & Computer Systems	$
PCs & Laptop Computers	$
Personal & Network Printers	$
Network Servers, Routers, Switches & Cables	$
Backup System & Supplies	$
Cash Registers	$
Internal System Monitors & Inventory Check Devices	$
Accounting System & Office Software	$
Payroll System	$
Computer System Maintenance Method	$
Postage System	$
Water Cooler & Coffee Machine	$
Stationary	$
Business Cards	$
Letterhead & Envelopes	$
Invoice & Statement Stock	$
Pick Tickets, Bill of Lading & Other Forms Stock	$
Office Supplies	$

First Aid Kit & Safety Supplies	$
Wall Clock	$
Corporate Fees	$
Activation Fees	$
Other:	$
Other:	$
Total Business Equipment & Supplies	$

Other Business Start-Up Expenses

Item	Estimate
Initial Inventory Stock	$
Freight In & Transportation Expenses	$
Company Vehicles	$
Marketing & Collateral Materials	$
Brochures, Specification & MSDS Sheets	$
Product Samples	$
Product Display Units	$
Promotional items	$
Pre-Opening Advertising	$
Pre-Opening Labor or Salaries	$
Temporary Agency & Other Hiring Fees	$
Other Local, State & Federal Compliance Costs	$
Owner & Employee Training	$
Dues & Subscriptions	$
Pre-Opening Travel Expenses	$
Conferences & Industry Meetings	$
Potential Customer Entertainment	$
Internet Name Registration & Web Site Fees	$
Moving Expenses	$
Employee Uniforms	$
Other Outside Services	$
Other:	$
Other:	$
Total Other Business Start-Up Expense	**$**

Total Business Start-Up Expense

Category	Estimate
Business Formation Expenses	$
Business Location Expenses	$
Manufacturing & Distribution Expenses	$
Business Equipment Expenses	$
Other Business Expenses	$
Total Start-Up Cost	**$**

Estimating Your Ongoing Business Costs

Starting a new business not only requires you to understand your start-up costs, but also the on-going operating and product costs. Without a clear picture of your cost, you can't hope to price your products correctly or understand if the market price will generate a profit for your business.

Similar to the start-up cost example, we'll identify the on-going and operational costs of operating a business. A little brainstorming and discussion with your advisors, coaches and other business owners in similar businesses will help you identify most of the expenses you can expect.

Analyze each expense line item to determine the least expensive method of acquiring your assets and services using the *Buy – Lease – Rent – Borrow* analysis. Keep these acquisition methods in mind as you go through the following sections to determine your on-going business costs.

These checklists are broken down into the following four categories:

1. Business Location Expenses
2. Manufacturing & Distribution Expenses
3. Office Equipment Expenses
4. Other Business Expenses

This is not meant to be a complete list of all possible expenses, but rather a good starting point. Many of these expenses will not apply to your business or industry. Some expenses are one-time and others are on-going. Use these lists to help you brainstorm all the potential expenses associated with running your business.

Ongoing Business Location Expenses

Item	Estimate
Building Occupancy Charges	$
Building Rent or Lease	$
Annual/Quarterly CAM Charges	$
Building Leasehold Improvements	$
Real Estate Taxes	$
Special School or Other Taxes	$
Snow Removal Assessments	$
Fire Dept. Inspection	$
Annual Sprinkler System & Fire Extinguisher Certification	$
Office Cleaning & Waste Removal	$
Insurance Expenses	$
Building & Contents Hazard Insurance	$
General Business Liability Insurance	$
Leased Equipment Coverage	$
Other Insurance:	$
Other Insurance:	$
Utilities	$
Electricity	$
Natural Gas	$
Heating Oil	$
Water	$
Sewer	$
Utility Co-Op Fees	$
Telephone	$
Trash & Rubbish Services	$
Other:	$
Total Business Location Expense	**$**

Ongoing Manufacturing/Distribution Equipment Expenses

Item	Estimate
Delivery Truck Expenses	$
Lease or Loan Payments	$
Vehicle Insurance	$
Taxes & Licenses	$
Driver Qualification & Training	$
Drug & Alcohol Testing Programs	$
Manufacturing & Fabrication Equipment	$
Equipment Maintenance	$
Insurance	$
Manufacturing Consumables	$
Manufacturing Storage	$
Product Station-to-Station Transportation	$
Tools	$
Warehouse Equipment	$
Forklift, Pallet Jacks & Hand Trucks	$
Dock Plates & Wheel Chocks	$
Warehouse Racks & Ladders	$
Fencing & Product Security	$
Conveyor Systems	$
RFID or SKU Identification System	$
Maintenance Supplies	$
Hand Tools	$
Warehouse Supplies	$
Safety Supplies	$
Fire Extinguishers	$
Rope, Twine & Product Containment Supplies	$
Paper Supplies	$
Shipping Supplies	$
Other:	$
Total Manufacturing/Distribution Expense	**$**

Onging Office Equipment & Supplies Expenses

Item	Estimate
Copy & Fax Machine Maintenance Contracts	$
Secure Recycling System Fees	$
Computers & Computer Systems	$
Network Maintenance & Updates	$
Personal & Network Printer Consumables	$
Backup System Supplies	$
Postage System Supplies & Postage	$
Water Cooler & Coffee Machine Supplies	$
Stationary	$
Business Cards	$
Letterhead & Envelopes	$
Invoice & Statement Stock	$
Pick Tickets, Bill of Lading & Other Forms Stock	$
Filing Supplies	$
Staplers, Tape & Tape Dispensers	$
Pens, Pencils, Markets, Hi-Liters, Other Office Supplies	$
First Aid Kit & Safety Supplies	$
Corporate Fees	$
Activation Fees	$
Other:	$
Other:	$
Total Business Equipment & Supplies Expense	**$**

Other Ongoing Business Expenses

Item	Estimate
Freight In & Transportation Expenses	$
Company Vehicle Expenses	$
Marketing & Collateral Materials	$
Brochures, Specification & MSDS Sheets	$
Product Samples	$
Product Display Units	$
Promotional items	$
Temporary Agency & Other Hiring Fees	$
Other Local, State & Federal Compliance Costs	$
Owner & Employee Training	$
Dues & Subscriptions	$
Pre-Opening Travel Expenses	$
Conferences & Industry Meetings	$
Customer Entertainment	$
Web Site Maintenance & Fees	$
Employee Uniforms	$
Other Outside Services	$
Employee Activities	$
Other:	$
Other:	$
Total Other Ongoing Business Expense	**$**

Total Ongoing Business Expenses

Category	Estimate
Business Location Expenses	$
Manufacturing & Distribution Expenses	$
Business Equipment Expenses	$
Other Business Expenses	$
Total Ongoing Cost	**$**

The Financial Statements

Creating financial statements can be the most intimidating part of the business planning process for many non-accountant owners. The terms aren't well understood and it seems more like a foreign language than a straightforward tool. This process really isn't that difficult and we'll walk through it here without the complicated and confusing terminology.

There are a few key points about financial statements that most potential business owners miss. This first is that they are tools for your use. Sure, if you get a bank loan you have to give a copy of your financial statements to your banker. But you are just giving the banker a copy of *your* reports. Don't think of these reports as requirements of the bank, think of them as requirements of the owner to properly manage a business.

The second point typically missed by entrepreneurs is that the financial statements are tools that help you measure the viability of your business model. An income statement and cash flow can help you distinguish between a passionate hobby and a viable business.

And third, financial statements are not living, breathing things. They are just reports that reflect the financial health and performance of your business. Don't mistake the reports for the business itself. The reports are just paper and ink. They should help you highlight those areas of your business where you need to work and those areas where your plan is coming together.

If you have an advisory board, make sure at least one of the advisors understands financial management. Have them work with you in this portion of the process to ensure your numbers make sense and the statements are put together correctly.

In this part, we'll look at the three main types of financial statements: the income statement, cash flow and, to a lesser extent, the balance sheet. For a start-up business, we'll be mostly concerned with projecting an income statement and a cash flow statement. Projecting a balance sheet is much more difficult to do for someone not familiar with accounting and probably not necessary at this stage for a start-up business.

Financial statements, whether historical or projected, are simply a numerical description of your business. An income statement tracks sales and expenses, a cash flow report measures the flow of cash and the balance sheet measures the relative size of assets (things you own) to liabilities (what you owe).

Details, Details, Details...

When setting up an accounting system, company owners struggle with how much detail to include in their account structure and statements. While there's no right or wrong answer, the important question to ask is how much detail do you need? You'll want to include as much detail as you need to manage your business. For example, you run an auto parts supply business and you supply local auto dealers. Part of your business includes making daily or in some cases twice daily deliveries of parts to area dealers. You might want to include more details about the cost of owning and operating your delivery fleet. Breaking out items such as fuel, service and other costs to operate your delivery function will help you evaluate the cost of that operation by being able to view the individual costs of that function. If you don't break out those costs individually, you'll not be able to track and measure that operation effectively and without measurement, you can't hope to make meaningful improvement.

The *Three Tools of Financial Viability*™

Entrepreneurs must determine before investing their own cash, borrowing cash from a bank or taking on an investor whether their business model is viable. For most small businesses, there are three basic financial tools that will serve to test the commercial viability of your business model. I call this analysis the *Three Tools of Financial Viability*™. The tools are:

V^1. The Income Statement

V^2. The Cash Flow Report

V^3. The Break-Even Analysis

The income statement tells you if your model will have a positive return, how big it will be and when it will happen. The cash flow report tells you how much cash it will take to fund this model and when, if ever, it starts generating a positive cash flow. Finally, the break-even analysis tells you how many units you have to sell to break even.

Prospective business owners should, at a minimum, use these three financial tools to determine if they should move forward with their plan. If any of these three basic finacial tools gives you an answer you don't like, go back to your model and make adjustments that result in different answers.

If you can't get the kind of results you expected or require and you can't modify your business model any further, it may be time to abandon this model and search for something else. Not every business model works. That's the beauty of these simple financial tools. You can test your model before investing your cash. If the model seems to work, then you can move forward. If the model doesn't work, you can tweak your model. If you can't tweak your model enough to make the kind of return you want, then do something else.

In the venture capital environment, investors look at dozens of models before finding one that works well enough for them to invest their cash. There's nothing wrong with determining that this particular model doesn't work. In fact, I consider that a win. If you can avoid losing your life's savings or declaring bankruptcy, that's a good step toward becoming a sucessful business owner.

The Income Statement

Sometimes referred to as the Profit and Loss Statement, the income statement measures the amount and timing of business profitability. That is, do you sell your goods or services for enough to cover the cost of producing those goods and services plus the regular cost of running your business and still have some left over. The statement is produced on a monthly, quarterly or yearly basis. For a small business, the statement has three sections: 1) sales, 2) the cost of your products or services and 3) the cost of running your business. A basic statement will look something like this:

> **Sales**
> **- Cost of Goods Sold**
> = Gross Margin
> **- Operating Expenses**
> = Net Income

Now, let's look at each of the three areas in more detail.

Sales – Sales, sometimes referred to as Revenue, are the total of the products or services that you sell to your customers less any returns or discounts taken during payment.

Cost of Goods Sold – Commonly referred to as COGS, the cost of goods sold are the costs associated with producing, fabricating, manufacturing, or acquiring what you sell. If your business is a manufacturing or similar operation, this section would include all costs associated with manufacturing or fabricating your products. If your building is used partially for manufacturing and partially for office, you can allocate that portion of the rent and utilities to manufacturing based on square feet used in each. You can use another method of splitting expenses, as long as it's reasonable and you use it consistently. You would also include labor associated with the production of those products. If you have office or clerical employees, you would not include their labor in the cost of goods sold section. The cost of goods sold expenses are the expenses directly related to producing your products.

Gross Margin – Gross profit margin or gross margin is the profitability from the product sales. In other words, gross margin is the base profitability of your product lines.

Operating Expenses – Cost of Operations is generally referred to as either General and Administrative (G&A) or Sales, General & Administrative (SG&A) expenses. These are the costs of running your business, such as rent, payroll, marketing expenses, insurance, selling expenses and utilities. In the start-up costs and ongoing expense worksheets, we explored most the costs associated with starting and running your business. Most of those costs will fall under operating expenses.

Net Income – Net income is the profitability from the entire operation. After deducting from the net sales all the costs of producing the product or service and then deducting all the costs of running your business on a monthly basis, what's left over is net income.

Service Business Income Statement Format

For a service business, you can use a slightly modified version of the income statement. Since you don't have any real cost of goods sold, you can omit that category of expense altogether. The format for a service business is:

> **Sales**
> **- Operating Expenses**
> = Net Income

In this case, you don't have to worry about categorizing expenses by operating or cost of goods.

Income Projections

The most difficult part of creating *projected* financial statements is estimating the sales volume. Start by considering all your research on your industry, competition, customers, and S.W.O.T. Anlysis. Then, with your marketing plan and product or service offering in mind, estimate how many widgets you will sell and at what price. This is probably *the* most difficult part of the whole business planning process. I wish I could give you a magic formula or even a magic wand that would give you a perfect estimate. No such magic exists.

Create an estimate and then discuss it with your advisors and coaches. While you should be in the best position to consider all the research and plans that you've completed, your advisors should be able to give you some reality check feedback. Carefully consider these estimates and make sure that they are based on solid research and marketing plans. These estimates are the critical piece in your whole financial projection model. If you get this wrong, everything else that follows will be wrong. Use your common sense and put on your best conservative thinking cap when making these projections.

Resist the temptation to overestimate your revenue to impress your advisors or banker. You are only fooling yourself. Remember, these financial statements are a tool to estimate the viability of your business model. Playing games with them will only hurt you. The income statement is the first of the *Three Tools of Financial Viability*™. If you determine that the model is in fact not viable, then go back and make changes to the model. Do not just tweak the income statement numbers. Make actual changes to the business model that result in different income statement outcomes. Think of the income statement as a statement of fact, over which you have no control. It is what it is. Of course you have significant control over the amount and type of expenses that you incur for your business. But the point is, estimate, to the best of your ability, the level of revenue and then let the expenses necessary to support that size business fall out appropriately.

Building an Income Statement

Start building your income statement projection by referring to your start-up expense worksheets and ongoing expense worksheets. Copy the expense categories appropriate for your business under the Cost of Goods Sold heading or the Operating Expense heading depending of the specific expense. If you are unsure of which category to place the expense, think about whether it is directly related to making the product. If it is, then place the expense category in the cost of goods area. If it's related to general business operations, place it in the operating expense area. Figure 1 shows the income statement format for Joe's Clean & Shine Car Wash. This is a simple income statement that shows the basic format for an income statement projection.

Create a column for each month in the year. You will have created a matrix with income and expense items vertically on the left side of the page with months horizontally across the page from left to right. After building your statement format with the appropriate expense items from your earlier brainstorming estimates, plug in your sales projections. Then, for each expense item, estimate the expense level based on the sales projection. Complete this exercise for each cost of good and operating expense item.

Joe's Clean & Shine Car Wash	
Year One Income Statement	
	Month
NET SALES	
Labor	
Water	
Supplies	
COST OF GOODS SOLD	
GROSS MARGIN	
Advertising	
Depreciation	
Insurance	
Rent	
Labor	
Telephone	
Utilities	
OPERATING EXPENSES	
NET INCOME	

Figure 1 - Income Statement Format

The Cash Flow Report

The cash flow report is different from a Statement of Cash Flows in that it is a projection of what is to come rather than a statement of fact of what has already happened. A Cash Flow Statement is an historical statement that shows where cash was used and generated in your business on a monthly, quarterly or yearly basis. It reconciles cash from the net income listed in your income statement and is typically only prepared by accountants.

The cash flow report is your best guess estimate of how your business will generate cash from sales and use cash in operations. For a small business, it's really not too difficult to complete. The cash flow report can be displayed in the same format as the income statement, but some of the category names are slightly different:

> **Cash Collections**
> **- Cost of Goods Sold**
> = Gross Cash Flow
> **- Operating Expenses**
> = Net Cash Flow

Cash Collections – Cash collections measures when and in what amounts cash flows into your bank account. If you sell in a retail setting for cash, check or credit card, you effectively get paid immediately. Credit card payments actually take a couple of days to settle, but for our purposes, that's pretty immediate. If you sell on open account with terms, you need to factor into your cash collections, when your customers will actually pay your invoices. For many businesses, this is the most difficult part of the cash forecasting process. However, if you break down your collections into the individual parts, you can set up a simple model in a spreadsheet to track your collections.

<u>Cost of Goods Sold</u> – In the same way that we spread our cash collected payments out over a couple of months by breaking those payments down into parts, we can do the same thing for our accounts payable, the invoices from our vendors. If you're paying your invoices by credit card or check as you receive the materials, then you're paying in the same month as you incur the expense. If you have payment terms, then just break down the payments into the month in which you'll be making payment. If you buy in this month and have Net 30 Days terms, then you'll record the outgoing payment in next month's column.

<u>Gross Cash Flow</u> – Gross cash flow is the result of subtracting cost of goods sold from cash collected.

<u>Operating Expenses</u> – Work your way down the income statement addressing each expense category individually and record the outgoing cash payment in the appropriate month. Most of your fixed expenses will be in this area and will be the same amount each month, like rent. Address each item asking when the actual cash will be paid.

<u>Net Cash Flow</u> – Subtracting the monthly cost of goods sold and operating expense cash expense from the monthly cash generated from collections will give the monthly net cash flow. Be sure to add an additional row where you calculate the cumulative cash flow over time. This figure will track how much cash your business generates or how much you'll have to borrow to keep your business operating.

Income Statement Category Name:	Cash Flow Report Category Name:
Net Sales	Cash Collected
Gross Margin	Gross Cash Flow
Net Income	Net Cash Flow

As we compare our income statement format to our cash flow report format, we can see that Net Sales becomes Cash Collected, Gross Margin becomes Gross Cash Flow and Net Income becomes Net Cash Flow. Notice that depreciation is not included in the cash flow report as it is not a cash item.

Joe's Clean & Shine Car Wash	
Cash Flow Report	
	Month
CASH COLLECTED	
Labor	
Water	
Supplies	
COST OF GOODS SOLD	
GROSS CASH FLOW	
Advertising	
Insurance	
Rent	
Labor	
Telephone	
Utilities	
OPERATING EXPENSES	
NET CASH FLOW	

Figure 2 – Cash Flow Report Format

It's important to recognize that the cash flow report only includes items that are cash. Any item on your income statement that is not cash should not be included in your cash flow report. Depreciation is only an accounting entry and not a real cash flow item, so it's not included on the cash flow report.

Depreciation should be calculated by your accountant. This figure represents the cost of replacing the asset over a period of its useful life. Useful life is a valuation term that means how long the item will be useful in your operation. The theory is that the item runs out of usefullness, or is used up over a period of time. For example, a new computer will only be useful to a business for a couple of years. After a couple of years, it will need to be replaced with a new machine. So the useful life of a computer may be only one to three years. A piece of manufacturing equipment may last much longer. Depending on the equipment, it may last for five to seven years. A building will likely last for over 20.

The amount of the monthly or yearly depreciation expense on your income statement is as much a function of the tax law as it is a function of the amount and item type. The Congress writes tax law and changes it every year. There are literally thousands of changes to the law each year. It makes no sense for you to spend your time trying to keep track of those changes. Leave that responsibility to the accountants. They are good at keeping track of these changes, let them manage it.

This whole issue of depreciation highlights one of the problems with an income statement; it's only an estimate. In fact, as your company gets bigger and more complex in its operations, the income statement becomes more and more of an estimate. It is not real! It's made up of estimates and accounting gimickery and cannot and should not be counted on as real numbers. That's why we create a cash flow report. A cash flow report is real. It measures how much money we can expect to have in our bank account in terms of real, hard currency.

Besides depreciation, the income statement, in an accrual based accounting world, assumes that certain large expenses will be spread out over the course of the year. For example, let's look at business insurance. Your business insurance expense may be $4,800 per year. For income statement purposes, we'll spread that cost over the course of the year at $400 per month. The total expense for the year hasn't changed, and the income statement is smoothed out. The larger the expense, the more important this smoothing is for reflecting our operations. While this sort of *smoothing* makes our income statement less like a real cash flow and less like reality, it makes for a more realistic picture of our business operations. The smoothed expenses are more reflective of how we use the expense than in the cash flow.

On a cash flow report, our $4,800 business insurance expense will in reality be paid in two payments of $2,400 each. That expense will be paid in advance in semi-annual installments. For example, the payment (that's cash!) might be due in January and July. For our cash flow report, the cash will leave our bank accounts and be reflected on the statement in two $2,400 payments, one in January and one in July. For the income statement, the $4,800 is shown as twelve $400 payments. The reality is two payments, the make believe is twelve payments. In their own statement, both are correct.

These differences are the reason that, as a small business owner, you must understand how the cash flow and income statements are different. More importantly, you need to understand how your actions in the real world are translated into profitability and cash flow in your business. As you study your actual financial reports each month, you'll become an expert in no time.

As you build a cash flow report, look at each income statement item and adjust which column the figures are in based on when the cash actually leaves your bank account. Like the $400 per month business insurance expense which will be shown as $2,400 payments in January and July, you'll need to adjust each expense item that is not reflective of how the cash actually changes hands.

The cash flow report is the entrepreneur's second of the *Three Tools of Financial Viability*™. This tool will estimate how much capital is required to start and maintain your business. Like the income statement tool, if you don't like the answer, then look back at your business model and determine what you can change to generate different results. Generally speaking, there aren't too many things you can realistically do to change your model. Other than delaying purchases and the method of acquiring assets, you're stuck with most of the model.

A key point to remember about cash flow versus profitability: you can operate your business at a loss for quite a while, depending on your level of resources. However, the day you run out of cash is the day you're out of business. You can't operate without cash. Cash is the lifeblood of a small business, indeed all business, and you can't stay in business without it.

<u>Monthly Format</u>

For business planning purposes, you'll want to work with a monthly format. In real life, cash flows on a daily basis. As you run your business and plan for your cash needs, you'll probably want to look at weekly cash flows as a management tool. Some businesses need to project on a daily basis to manage and reduce their borrowing costs. Depending on your business, you can manage your cash flows on a basis that makes sense for your situation. However, for business planning, a monthly cash flow format will suffice.

You should figure on projecting your income statement and cash flow report for at least 2 to 3 years, by month. While a projection over two years is generally not very accurate, it's important to show to yourself as well as to others who might have a vested financial interest in your business (like your banker) how your business model will perform over time. How long will it take you to get over the initial hump to profitability? How much business and over what period of time will be required before your business becomes a viable operation?

This is a big part of the viability equation. If your business will take several years to become profitable, keep adding additional years until you determine how long it will take. If it takes 4+ years to reach profitability, then you'd better have significant start-up capital. For most entrepreneurs, I would question the true viability of the business model if it takes more than three years to reach profitability. I'm not saying that it's not possible for an excellent long-term company to take a few years to become profitable, especially if it's in a technology, biology or research field. But most small business start-ups aren't in those fields and their model will need to be profitable earlier rather than later if they hope to have a chance of surviving. If your model requires a long break-even time frame, make sure you have good advisors reviewing your model and confirming your assumptions and projections.

Break-Even Analysis

Break-even is one of the most commonly used methods for evaluating a new business enterprise or new product line or manufacturing facility. It's a tool for analyzing how sales revenue, profit and expenses vary with changes in one of the variables. The break-even point is an equilibrium where sales revenue is equal to costs. At the break-even point, no profits are earned and no losses are incurred. Break-even is a cash flow tool (so we will not consider non-cash expenses in the calculation) that is easy to calculate. It is widely used in production management and by cost and management accountants and can prove useful in determining whether to make an investment in a new plant, a specific piece of equipment or a whole business entity.

The break-even analysis is the entrepreneur's third tool of the *Three Tools of Financial Viability*™.

One of the drawbacks of the break-even analysis is the assumption that nothing changes. That is, the model assumes that the conditions that were present during the calculation do not change. Of course, everything changes constantly. Sales prices are affected by overall sales volume and costs of raw materials, labor and transportation costs. Therefore, the break-even must be recalculated as changes occur to the components driving your business.

In order to compute the break-even point, we need to know the following variables:

- Annual Sales
- Gross Profit Margin
- Operating Expenses (less depreciation)
- Annual Debt Service

With these figures in hand, we can caluate the various components of break-even.

Break-Even Sales:

$$\frac{(Operating\ Expenses + Annual\ Debt\ Service)}{Gross\ Profit\ Margin\ \%}$$

Break-Even Gross Margin:

$$\frac{(Operating\ Expenses + Annual\ Debt\ Service)}{Annual\ Sales}$$

Break-Even Operating Expenses:

$$Annual\ Sales \times Gross\ Profit\ Margin\ \%$$

Break-Even Worksheet

Using the following data for a ficticious company, calculate the break-even components.

Annual Sales:	$1,000,000
Gross Profit:	250,000
Operating Expenses:	170,000
Debt Payment:	2,500

Break-Even Sales:

$$\frac{\text{Operating Expenses} + \text{Annual Debt Service}}{\text{Gross Margin \%}}$$

Break-Even Margin:

$$\frac{\text{Operating Expenses} + \text{Annual Debt Service}}{\text{Sales}}$$

Break-Even Operating Expenses:

Annual Sales × Gross Margin %

Break-Even Worksheet – Answer Sheet

Break-Even Sales:

$$\frac{\text{Operating Expenses} + \text{Annual Debt Service}}{\text{Gross Margin \%}}$$

Operating Expenses = \$170,000
Annual Debt Service = \$2,500 × 12 = \$30,000
Gross Margin % = \$250,000 ÷ \$1,000,000 = .25 × 100 = 25%

(\$170,000 + \$30,000) ÷ 25% = \$200,000 ÷ .25 = **\$800,000**

Break-Even Margin:

$$\frac{\text{Operating Expenses} + \text{Annual Debt Service}}{\text{Sales}}$$

Operating Expenses = \$170,000
Annual Debt Service = \$2,500 × 12 = \$30,000

(\$170,000 + \$30,000) ÷ \$1,000,000 = \$200,000 ÷ \$1,000,000 = 0.20 = **20.0%**

Break-Even Operating Expenses:

Sales × Gross Margin %

Gross Margin % = \$250,000 ÷ \$1,000,000 = .25 × 100 = 25%

\$1,000,000 × 25% = \$1,000,000 × .25 = **\$250,000**

The Balance Sheet

The balance sheet is a summary of what the business owns and what it owes, at a particular point in time. The difference between what a business owns and owes, is the owner's equity. Let's look at a sample balance sheet and discuss the different components.

In the left-hand column (or top group shown here) are the assets. Assets are the things your business owns, like cash in bank accounts, accounts receivable, your inventory, buildings and equipment. You notice that these assets are divided into 'current' and 'long-term' assets. The balance sheet distinguishes in both the assets and liabilities columns between short-term or 'current' items and long-term items. The cut-off is generally one year. So, a short-term asset is one that can be converted to cash within one year. For liabilities, it's debt that must be repaid in less than one year. Debts that are due over a longer time period are classified as long-term liabilities. Same for assets such as building and equipment, they will be used over a long time period, versus items that will be used or converted in less than one year.

In the right hand column (or bottom group) are the liabilities and shareholders' equity. Liabilities include items such as accounts payable, lines of credit, and bank loans. The difference between the total assets and total liabilities is the owners' equity or shareholders' equity. Shareholders' equity is comprised of such items as common stock, paid-in capital and retained earnings.

Joe's Clean & Shine Car Wash

Sample Balance Sheet

ASSETS

Current Assets		
Cash	$	83
Accounts Receivable		1,312
Inventory		1,270
Other Current Assets		85
Total Current Assets	**$**	**2,750**
Net Property, Plant & Equipment		2,230
Other Assets		213
Total Assets	**$**	**5,193**

LIABILITIES & EQUITY

Liabilities		
Currrent Liabilities		
Accounts Payable	$	1,022
Credit Line		100
Current Portion LTD		52
Total Current Liabilities	**$**	**1,174**
Long Term Debt		1,037
Other L-T Liabilities		525
Total Liabilities	**$**	**2,736**
Equity		
Common Stock	$	74
Additional Paid-In-Capital		1,110
Retained Earnings		1273
Total Equity	**$**	**2,457**
Total Liabilities & Equity	**$**	**5,193**

Figure 2 – Sample Balance Sheet

Generally speaking, it is very difficult to construct a balance sheet without the help of an accountant. Your job as an entrepreneur and hopeful business owner is to construct the projected income statement and cash flow report. Work with your accountant to estimate year end balance sheets. The creation of balance sheet estimates is beyond the scope of this book and the expertise of most beginning business owners. However, your accountant or other advisor knowledgeable in accounting will be able to assist you with this statement.

Growth and Cash Flow

Growth is the number one goal of most small entrepreneurs and cash flow difficulties are typically the number one result of unplanned and uncontrolled growth. Growth requires capital. If you're having cash flow problems now, growing will only make that worse. Significant growth requires careful planning, attention to captial requirements as well as lender and creditor relations.

Growth Requires Capital.

As a business grows, there are threshold levels at which the current business infrastructure can support revenue. At your current infrastructure level, your business can support a range of revenue levels. Once you approach and surpass the upper limit of that range, new amounts of infrastructure will have to be added to your business to support any increases in revenue. Once you add new infrastructure, though, you can support a new range of revenue. The point is to approach but not surpass an infrastructure requirement level of revenue until you are ready. New levels of infrastructure also require cash and therefore should be planned and not added only by necessity or in an unplanned manner. Large increases in infrastructure may require support from your primary lender.

Growing your business with low margin sales may not increase profits enough to warrant the extra work and risk. Likewise, sales that require high service requirements may end up lowering your profits. After all, that's what this game is all about: generating profits that you can put in your pocket. Growth in your company can sometimes create more hassles than it's worth

Typically only debt financing is available to support sales growth. To repay debt, the company must generate more sales, which requires more debt. It's a vicious cycle from which many companies cannot escape. If your bank will not provide the credit necessary to support growth, credit will have to come from suppliers. Supplier credit can come in the form of intentionally increased credit limits and payment terms, or unintentionally with a slowdown in payments.

Use extreme caution in accepting a temporary increase in credit terms. If you normally pay your vendors in 30-days, they may offer a 'temporary' increase in terms to say, 60-days or 90-days, to *assist* you with growth. If the vendor is supplying the product to generate the growth, they may actually think they are helping. In fact, they are creating a situation in which you will likely never recover. If you only have the cash flow to pay one month's worth of vendor invoices per month, you will have to double or triple up when the special terms end. To bring your vendor account from 60-days to 30-days, you'll have to pay two months worth of invoices in one month. Most businesses are unable to generate this much cash flow and therefore will be unable to reign in these *temporary* terms once the promotion is over.

Measuring Performance

Now that your financial projections are completed or your company has been in business for a while and is generating regular financial statements, how do you know if you are doing well or just getting by? Do you have a yardstick with which to measure your progress or projections? How do you know if your projections are good and your banker or investor will look at them favorably?

As you work on your business and strive to improve your performance, what measurements will you use? Can you know within a high degree of certainty whether you *should* think positively about your results? How do you know? You simply measure your results against the standard results of your industry. This information is catalogued and recorded by a couple of companies, the Risk Management Association (formerly Robert Morris Associates) in the ***Annual Statement Studies*** and Dr. Leo Troy in the ***Almanac of Business and Industrial Financial Ratios***. Both of these publications list industry categories by NAICS code. The data is presented for the income statement and selected financial ratios by revenue size and asset size categories. You can use this information to compare your performance against your industry. Use industry data to measure your progress and get an indication of whether your success is average or exceptional.

But how do you know what to measure? Which ratios are right for your business? There are literally hundreds of financial and operational ratios and measures available plus any number that you and your team make up for your particular use. What you use depends on your business and how you operate. A careful analysis of your business and its operations will guide you in selecting operational measures. In the Using Financial Ratios section later in this section, I have selected a core group of financial ratios that make sense for most privately held small businesses. You can't measure everything or you end up doing nothing but measuring and not making any improvement. Pick the operational measures that make sense and get on with it. Over time, the measures or categories may change in importance as you fine tune certain processes and your business changes. Continue to evaluate and prioritize the most important measurements and use them to actively manage your business processes and finances.

Using Financial Ratios

The historical financial statements; income statement, balance sheet and statement of cash flows, offer a glimpse into the financial health of a company. As we discussed earlier, it is important to understand that these financial statements are in many ways, just an estimate of the actual performance. For example, we record revenue at the moment the sales invoice is generated, often without regard to whether the invoice will actually be paid. Many other balance sheet items are also estimates of the actual performance of an individual asset or liability. Usually, the performance difference between the estimate and actual is small and has relatively little bearing on the bottom line. Sometimes, the difference is substantial.

It is often challenging to get a complete picture of a company's financial health by just looking at the financials. It's difficult to compare past performance to current performance by only looking at these statements. Financial ratios offer a short-cut to understanding financial performance. Ratios are especially good at creating trends of performance and comparing one company to another or to an industry average.

Financial ratios simply indicate the relationship of one number to another. They are easily calculated by dividing one number by another and expressing the result as either a percentage or a number of times relationship. The beauty of financial ratios is that they provide comparisons that reveal more about the financial health of the company than just the numbers in the financial statements alone.

Within each category of ratios, there are dozens of formalized ratios used by various groups or agencies. Many of these ratios are specifically geared towards public companies and very large companies. As my practice is primarily involved with smaller private companies, I have consolidated those hundreds of ratios into eleven ratios that I believe are most appropriate for small and medium sized privately held companies. These ratios are easy to calculate from standard published financial statements and are best if used over time. That is, they reveal the most when looked at in a trend over several years. However, many of these ratios can also be used with your projected financial statements.

The interpretation of financial ratios can be skewed by the intentional mismanagement of a company's financial statements. The CFOs who participate in this sort of activity usually make the news and have unhappy futures. Offering interpretations in the individual ratio listings for such cases would make this guide long and unnecessarily complicated. This information is offered as a tool for small and medium sized business owners to evaluate the performance of their own company. The guide assumes that management is using its best efforts to run a business in a legal and ethical manner.

Protifability Ratios

Profitability ratios measure a company's ability to generate profits and control expenses.

Gross Profit Margin Percentage

Computation: gross profit (revenue minus cost of goods sold) divided by revenue.

Gross Margin % = Gross Profit ÷ Revenue

Interpretation: Gross Margin % shows the profitability of the company's products or services themselves, without other overhead expenses. This ratio can be applied to the company as a whole or all the way down to a specific product or SKU. It is a key measure of profitability, because it is difficult to increase the gross margin of a product. On a trend basis, an increase in the gross margin reflects the company's ability to pass along raw material increases to the customer or may be an indication that they are facing little competition or have a superior sales force. Decreasing gross margins indicate that the company is under severe competitive pressures and is having to lower its prices to generate sales or that it's not able to pass along increases in raw materials or labor wage increases. As such, the gross margin serves as an early warning signal of the company's health.

Net Profit Margin Percentage

Computation: net profit divided by revenue.

Net Profit Margin % = Net Profit ÷ Revenue

Interpretation: Net Profit Margin %, also known as return on sales, reflects the company's bottom line performance. It tells how much profit a company gets to keep after paying all the bills. Like the other two profit margin ratios, the net profit margin percent is best considered in a trend and compared to companies in a similar industry or industry averages by company size.

Return on Assets (ROA)

Computation: net profit divided by total assets

Return on Assets = Net Profit ÷ Total Assets

Interpretation: This ratio expresses the return on total assets and measures the effectiveness of management in employing the resources available to it. It expresses the percentage of every dollar invested in the business that was returned to the owner as profit. It also allows for the comparison of company performance across size categories. While a high percentage is good, a ROA that is too high may reflect profits being stripped from the company and not being reinvested for future profits. If a company doesn't continue investing in new assets, its long-range profitability will suffer.

Return on Equity (ROE)

Computation: net Profit divided by Shareholder's Equity

Return on Equity = Net Profit ÷ Shareholder's Equity

Interpretation: This ratio expresses the rate of return on invested capital. While it can serve as an indicator of management performance, you are cautioned to use it in conjunction with other ratios. A high return, normally associated with effective management, could indicate an under-capitalized business. Whereas, a low return, usually an indicator of inefficient management performance, could reflect a highly capitalized, conservatively operated business. In any event, it's a good indication of whether a company is capable of returning a profit that is worth the risk.

Leverage Ratios

Leverage ratios let you see how extensively a company uses debt, or leverage, in its operations. Leverage ratios refer to financial leverage, the extent to which a company's assets are financed with debt, as compared to operating leverage, which is the ratio of fixed costs to variable costs. Bankers love the leverage ratios.

Debt-to-Equity

Computation: total liabilities divided by shareholder's equity

Debt-to-Equity = Total Liabilities ÷ Shareholder's Equity

Interpretation: This ratio expresses the relationship between capital contributed by creditors and that contributed by owners. It is simply the ratio of how much debt the company has for every dollar of shareholder equity. The higher the ratio, the greater the risk being assumed by creditors. A lower ratio generally indicates greater long-term financial safety. A firm with a low debt-to-equity ratio usually has greater flexibility to borrow in the future. A more highly leveraged company has a more limited debt capacity.

Interest Coverage

Computation: operating profit divided by annual interest charges

Interest Coverage = Operating Profit ÷ Annual Interest Charges

Interpretation: This ratio measures the company's interest exposure; how much of its operating profit is needed just to cover the annual interest expense. A ratio of 1.0 means that all the company's operating profits are required just to pay the interest expense. A high ratio generally means that a company can afford to take on more debt.

Liquidity Ratios

Liquidity ratios reveal a company's ability to meet its financial obligations including debt, payroll, taxes and payments to vendors.

<u>Current Ratio</u>

Computation: current assets divided by current liabilities

Current Ratio = Current Assets ÷ Current Liabilities

Interpretation: This ratio is a rough indication of a firm's ability to service its current obligations in the short term. Generally, the higher the current ratio, the greater the "cushion" between current obligations and a firm's ability to pay them. A ratio less than 1.0 means that the company will run out of cash to meet its obligations in the short term. The composition and quality of current assets is a critical factor in the analysis of an individual firm's liquidity.

<u>Quick Ratio</u>

Computation: current assets minus inventory divided by current liabilities.

Quick Ratio = (Current Assets - Inventory) ÷ Current Liabilities

Interpretation: Also known as the "ACID TEST" ratio, it is a refinement of the current ratio and is a more conservative measure of liquidity. The ratio expresses the degree to which a company's current liabilities are covered by the most liquid assets. Generally, any value of less than 1.0 implies a reciprocal "dependency" on inventory or other current assets to liquidate short-term debt.

Efficiency Ratios

The efficiency ratios show how efficiently management runs certain base functions of the company; inventory, collections and payables.

<u>Days Inventory</u>

Computation: average inventory or ending inventory divided by cost of goods sold per day

Days Inventory = Ending Inventory ÷ (Cost of Goods Sold ÷ 360)

Interpretation: measures how many days of inventory are in the production or distribution system. Inventory flows through a company's 'system' at a faster or slower rate, how fast it moves is an indication of how quickly the company can turn inventory into cash. Both the Days Inventory and the Inventory turns measure how efficiently a company utilizes its inventory.

Inventory Turns is a function of Days Inventory in that it measures how many times a company's inventory turns over during a year. It is calculated by dividing the days inventory into 360.

Inventory Turns = 360 ÷ Days Inventory

<u>Days Sales Outstanding (DSO)</u>

Computation: ending accounts receivable (A/R) divided by revenue per day

Days Sales Outstanding = Ending A/R ÷ (Revenue ÷ 360)

Interpretation: DSO is a measure of how quickly a company's customers pay their bills. Generally, the greater number of days outstanding, the greater the probability of delinquencies in accounts receivable. A comparison of a company's daily receivables may indicate the extent of a company's control over credit and collections. The terms offered by a company to its customers may differ from terms within the industry and should be taken into consideration.

Days Payables Outstanding (DPO)

Computation: ending accounts payable (A/P) divided by cost of goods sold per day

Days Payables Outstanding = Ending A/P ÷ (Cost of Goods Sold ÷ 360)

Interpretation: This figure expresses the average time in days that it takes a company to pay its vendors. Generally, the higher the number, the more cash a company is keeping on hand. However, the company has to strike a balance between preserving cash and keeping vendors happy.

```
┌─────────────────────────────────────────────────┐
│               Financial Ratios Worksheet         │
└─────────────────────────────────────────────────┘
```

Using the data from your financial projections in your business plan, calculate the following financial ratios for your business.

Profitability Ratios

Gross Profit Margin %: _____ ÷ _____ = _____

Net Profit Margin %: _____ ÷ _____ = _____

Return on Assets: _____ ÷ _____ = _____

Return on Equity: _____ ÷ _____ = _____

Leverage Ratios

Debt-to-Equity: _____ ÷ _____ = _____

Interest Coverage: _____ ÷ _____ = _____

Liquidity Ratios

Current Ratio: _____ ÷ _____ = _____

Quick Ratio: (_____ - _____) ÷ _____ = _____

Efficiency Ratios

Days Inventory: _____ ÷ (_____ ÷ 360) = _____

Inventory Turns: 360 ÷ _____ = _____

Days Sales Outstanding (DSO): _____ ÷ (_____ ÷ 360)

   = _____

Days Payable Outstanding (DPO):   _____ ÷ (_____ ÷

   360) = _____

Industry Financial Ratios Worksheet

Using the data from the RMA Annual Statement Studies from your local university library, compare your company financial ratios with those from your industry and revenue size.

Ratio Name	Company	Industry

Profitability Ratios

Gross Profit Margin %:   _____   _____

Net Profit Margin %:   _____   _____

Return on Assets: _____   _____

Return on Equity: _____   _____

Leverage Ratios

Debt-to-Equity: _____   _____

Interest Coverage: _____   _____

Liquidity Ratios

Current Ratio: _____   _____

Quick Ratio: _____   _____

Ratio Name	Company	Industry

Efficiency Ratios

Days Inventory: _____   _____

Days Sales Outstanding (DSO): _____   _____

Days Payable Outstanding (DPO): _____   _____

Discuss each of the ratio comparisons and determine if you are better or worse than the industry figure. What might you do to change your business operations to improve your financial performance?

Profitability Ratios

Leverage Ratios

Liquidity Ratios

Efficiency Ratios

Financial Statement Case Study

Use the following assumptions to create an income statement and cash flow report for the Widget Distribution Company, LLC located in Huntsville, Alabama.

Widget Distribution Company, LLC (WDC) sells widgets out of a storefront in a strip center that it rents for $400 per month. It pays utilities of $75 per month and business insurance of $648 in March of each year, but smoothes the expense on its income statement, accruing $54 monthly. WDC pays dues to its trade association of $300 per year in January, and like the insurance, accrues the expense at $25 per month. WDC has one employee who earns $10 per hour. In addition, they have payroll tax and benefits expense of 18% of gross payroll. Assume that all payroll expenses are paid as earned. Payroll hours vary with sales volume and are shown on the table below.

WDC sells its widgets for $25 each to the general population who pay in cash or credit card at the point of purchase and to industrial concerns to which it grants terms of 1% 10 Days, Net 30 Days. Retail sales represent 20% of the total sales and industrial sales the remaining 80%. Of the industrial sales, 30% take the cash discount, 60% pay in 30 days and 10% pay in 60 days.

WDC buys its stock from Widgets USA, Inc. in Indianapolis, Indiana at $8.75 each. The widgets come 10 units to a case and have a $2.50 per case freight charge from the factory in Indiana to the storefront in Alabama. WDC receives terms on its purchases from Widgets USA, Inc. of 1% 10 Days, Net 30 Days. They pay in 30 days.

Use the information contained above and in the table following to complete a projected income statement and cash flow report.

Month	# Widgets Sold	Labor Hours Worked
January	110	126
February	120	120
March	150	132
April	160	132
May	180	136
June	210	143
July	220	154
August	230	147
September	240	154
October	250	165
November	250	160
December	260	168

Case Study Summary

Based on the income statement and cash flow report that you created, answer the following questions:

1. Is Widget Distribution Company, LLC a profitable company?
2. Do they ever lose money?
3. What is the gross margin percent?
4. If the owners had $5,000 of start-up capital, would they need to borrow money?
5. What month does the cash flow turn positive?

The projected income statement and cash flow report are tools for the prospective owner to use to measure the performance of their business plan. If the owner doesn't like the results indicated, the business plan should be modified to change the indicated results. Understand that you can't say 'I'm going to increase sales by 12%' without having substantive plans to do so. Willing it so is rarely a viable business strategy. If you need to make a substantial change to your results, then you need to make a change to your plan backed up with real action that will garner the results you wish.

After making changes to your plan, use the projected income statement and cash flow report to indicate the results. In this way, it becomes clear how these two financial tools can be used to create the results you desire. Remember, realistic results require realistic thinking and plans. Use your advisors to help you do a reality check at this point in your business planning process.

Part 5: Writing the Business Plan

"I'm just preparing my impromptu remarks."

—Winston Churchill

Business Plans

One of the most difficult projects for new business owners seems
to be writing a business plan. The process is really quite
straightforward, but it causes many sleepless nights and nervous
days for would-be entrepreneurs. Writing a business plan can be
broken down into subparts, making the job a more reasonable
mountain to climb. And while new research done at the
University of Maryland's business school suggests that venture
capitalists no longer read business plans, but instead rely almost
entirely on their 'gut feeling', you should still give this project
your best effort. Most new business owners will not be presenting
their idea to venture capitalists, and those that will, need all the
practice they can get.

The business plan document represents a summary of your plans,
research and expected performance of your business. It is
presented in a format that makes for easy reading for bankers and
other outsiders. The business plan is just a summary of what
you've learned about the industry, competition, customer and
your plan to make a profit. It's really no more complicated than
that. At this point in the process you should have already done
the research and made many of the important decisions. Now it's
time to write them down.

How detailed your writing style will depend on your business. If
you're a small business with only meager cash needs, you can
probably get away with simple paragraphs and bulleted lists for
most items. If your business is complicated and requires
significant funding, sharpen your pencil. You don't have to be a

published author to write a business plan. Only the most complicated businesses and those with significant cash needs should have a lengthy plan. Most businesses can get by with a short business plan write-up supplemented with supporting documentation and financials.

After you've completed your plan and created your financial projections, how do you know if the results are good? Without a yardstick for measuring your results, you'll not have a clue whether your results are good, average or poor. The basic profitable/not profitable decision is easy, but I'm assuming you want to do better than just break even. We looked at performance yardsticks for measuring the results of your business and how to improve your financial results in Part 4 of this book.

Types of Business Plans

While there are as many types of business plans as there are types of businesses, I generally break down business plan types into three categories: Formal, Informal and Summary.

Formal

A formal business plan is what most entrepreneurs think of as a business plan. It should be the most comprehensive and detailed form of your plan. The purpose of the formal plan is for presentation to bankers, investors or other partners of the business. While all business plans are summaries of the research, conclusions, goals and objectives, the formal plan gives the most detail. These individuals will need the detailed analysis of the industry, competition, customer and SWOT analysis as well as financial projections. The analysis will typically be presented as a narrative with the addition of charts, graphs and tables to help illustrate the data where appropriate.

Informal

An informal business plan summarizes the same research, conclusions, goals and objectives as the formal plan, but in a more summarized fashion. This type plan is typically used for the management team to guide planning and budgeting and lead the performance measurement thinking of this group. The management team was most likely involved in the preparation of the plan and doesn't need the detail. They may not need any mention at all of the description of the business section. Who the corporate attorney is and what type of bookkeeping system is in place is really wasted copy for this group. They need the appropriate detail in the strategic sections of the overall plan.

Summary

The summary business plan is typically used for marketing purposes where detailed information about the company would not be appropriate. It might be used as a recruitment tool for potential employees or to give vendors and other business partners an indication of the overall goals and plans of the company. Confidential information would not be included in this type of plan.

The type of plan you use will depend on the situation and the audience. It is important to understand though, that the research, conclusions, goals and objectives are completed before writing the plan and do not change based on the type of plan you write. The proper research and planning is necessary to run a successful operation and doesn't change based on your plan type.

Business Plan Template

A quick search of the Internet will garner you more examples of a business plan than you'll ever need. There are some excellent examples of business plans in hundreds of locations easily found with a search. There is business plan software in a range of prices from $19.95 and up. However, you don't need software or a fancy plan document. You can use my example format or any of the ones you find on the Internet. It just doesn't matter that much. The important thing is that you cover the items that are important to *your* business. No software or template can tell you that. With that said, here's a sample table of contents that you can use as a starting point.

Executive Summary

Organization

Industry & Markets

Marketing Plan

Financial Analysis & Projected Financials

Addenda

A detailled business plan template follows with many of the items listed for a generic business. If you choose to use this format, add any additional items that are required for your business or delete the ones that don't apply.

ple Business Plan Template

195

Summary

Organization

✓ Description of Business
✓ Products & Services
✓ Location
✓ Owners & Management Team
　　Who Are They?
　　Why Are They Qualified?
　　Board of Director's or Advisory Board
✓ Organization Chart p· ʳ|7
✓ Legal Structure
　　Employee Recruitment & Retention
　　Recordkeeping
　　Professional Relationships
　　　　Attorney
　　　　Banker
　　　　CPA/Accountant
　　　　Insurance Agent
　　　　Consultant
　　　　Other Professional Advisors

Industry & Markets

Industry
　　✓ Description of Industry
　　✓ Industry Trends
　　　Laws & Rules Applying to Your Industry
　　　Special Industry Considerations
　　　　　Capital Restraints

Environmental Issues
✓Ease/Difficulty of Entering Industry

✓Market Segments
Brief Description of Major Market Segments
Detailed Description of Your Market Segment
Special Market Segment Considerations

Competition
✓List Competition (Direct & Indirect)
✓Brief Description of Direct Competitors
Company Name & Locations
Description of Product or Service
Strengths & Weaknesses
People
Capital
Technology
Intellectual Property
Market Position
History
Location

✓Customers
Who Are They?
Where Do They Live & Work?
Where Do They Play?
How Much $ Do They Make?
Define Using WHATEVER Socio-Demo-Geo-
Characteristic Is Important

✓Company
Strengths
Weaknesses
Opportunities
Threats

Marketing Plan

✓ Market Situation Analysis
       Define the Market
       Identify the Target
       Unique Value Proposition/Unique Selling
         Proposition
       Brand
✓ Marketing Strategy
       Budget
       Goals (Market Objectives)
       Timetable
       Resources Needed
       Monitor/Measure/Test

✓ Implementation Tactics
       Action Plan
       Specific Advertising & Promotion Campaigns
       PR Campaigns
       Networking & Professional Organizations

Financial Analysis & Projected Financials

✓ Financial & Sales Goals
✓ Resources Needed
       Capital Equipment
       Start-Up Costs
       Marketing Collateral
       Product Samples
✓ Summary of Financial Need
✓ Projected Income Statement
       Projected Balance Sheet
       Cash Flow Report
       Break Even Analysis
       Ratio Analysis with Industry Standards
    Financial Projection Assumptions

Addenda

Management Resumes
Owners Personal Financial Statement
Owners Tax Returns
Legal Documents
    Articles of Organization
    Operating Agreement
    Real Estate & Equipment Lease Agreements
    Other Loan or Financing Agreements
    Patents
    Manufacturing Agreements
    IRS Taxpayer ID
    Patents
    Building & Equipment Leases
    Management Agreements
    Licenses & Permits
    Non-Compete Agreements
Other Pertinent Documents
    Product or Service Information
    Relevant Market Information
    Product Brochures
    Published Articles and White Papers
    Product Pictures
    Product Samples
    Product MSDS Sheets
    Product License Agreements
    Health & Safety Information
Market Studies
Competitor Marketing Information
Trade Journal & Magazine Articles
3rd Party Market Research

This outline can be used and added to or subtracted from, depending on your business. How much or how little you say depends on your business and your audience. Keep in mind that a business plan is a summary of your business, market and industry research, products and services, goals and financial projections.

Writing a Business Plan

Executive Summary

The executive summary is a one-page summary of your plan. It should include a brief statement of your financial need. Many individuals will only read this page and skip ahead to the financial statements. Take a little time to get this page right. You have to condense your whole business plan down into a page or at most, two pages. If you have only one page to make or break your business plan, what would you say?

Overview of Organization

This section will tell your readers who you are, what you'll make and who will do the making. You will want to include at least a sentence about the topics listed including legal structure. You may want to include information about how you will account for the business (i.e. accounting software vs. MS Excel), if you're using an accounting firm, attorney, insurance broker and so forth.

Ownership information should be included in your business plan including the names of owners, their ownership interest and proposed involvement in the business. Do they have any expertise in a business like the one you are proposing? In addition, you'll want to include a section on the management of your business. Who are the individuals and what is their expertise? How will these individuals help you achieve success?

If you have a board of directors or an advisory board, discuss their specific skills and how they will help you.

This portion of the business plan is very straightforward and can be completed quickly. At this point, you should already know all this information.

Market Analysis

The market analysis gets into the meat of your business plan. The market analysis section should reflect your understanding of the market in which you plan to operate. You should include data in this section about the size of the market, its growth expectations, trends, technology developments and so forth.

Within the overall market, what are the different industries? How much volume and in what parts of the world, country or state do they come into play? Understanding the size and trends in your specific industry is crucial to your success. How much of your industry's total volume do you plan to take? What percentage of the total will you represent?

Who is your competition? What is their market share? What do they do well? What do they do poorly? To the extent that you know or can find through research, I like to do a S.W.O.T. (**S**trengths, **W**eaknesses, **O**pportunities and **T**hreats) analysis on each major competitor. This sort of thinking can help you fine-tune your product or service offering to take advantage of a niche that may not be adequately covered by your competitors. You need to understand what products and services your competitors offer and at what price. It is difficult to get all this type of info on your competitors, especially if they are small businesses without any public filings. However, at a minimum, you should look at strengths and weaknesses of your competition and determine how those strengths and weaknesses present opportunities and threats to your business.

Strategic Analysis

The strategic analysis should center on your company S.W.O.T. analysis. Like in the previous section where you did a simple analysis on your competitors, you should do a detailed and thorough analysis of your business. On what basis do you plan to compete with the other companies already offering the same product or service in the market? Is your product or service new? Have you developed a new way of approaching an old problem? While these may be true, it's unlikely. If you're using advisors, this would be a good time to have them do a reality check.

Think you don't have any competitors? Think again! I've never seen a start-up yet without any competition. Sometimes competition comes from unusual sources, like an existing company in another industry or business that springs to life when they see a market opportunity. Sometimes competition comes from the Internet in the form of an on-line company with no physical presence in your market. Whether from a direct, indirect or purely on-line source, every business has competition.

Marketing Plan

Other areas to discuss are your marketing and advertising plan. How will you go to market and what is your strategy for growing your business? What are your distribution channels and how will you leverage your strengths to improve your success? What is your marketing and communication budget and how will this plan unfold?

What are your product or service offerings? What makes your products or services different from those already in the market?

What is your pricing and how does it compare to your
competitors and what is your pricing strategy? What are your
R&D plans and are any of your products or services covered by
patents or copyrights?

Financial Analysis

In the financial analysis section, you'll want to discuss your need
for funds and how you'll repay those funds. You will also need to
discuss the assumptions that go into your financial statements.
This is a section that lends itself to bullets. What information does
your reader need to know in order to fully understand your
financial statements? What are your sales goals? Where will you
get and how much will you pay for your raw materials? How
much is your labor cost and other overhead expenses?

The second part of this section should include your projected
financial statements. You should include at a minimum, 2 – 3
years worth of profit and loss statements and cash flow reports.
Depending on your business type, you may also need projected
balance sheets. You may need advisory or even professional
assistance generating your financial statements if you're
unfamiliar with how the statements work or even how to read a
financial statement. If you need help, get it. Sloppy work here
can spell disaster for your financial future and give your banker or
other outside readers little confidence in your abilities.

If you have an existing business and plan investment in new
equipment or infrastructure, you'll need to explain how the
investment will be made and what you expect to get in return and
under what time frame. A return on investment analysis or ROI
will calculate the percentage return you expect to achieve from the
investment.

Addenda

The addenda section will vary depending on the reader and their requirements. If you're preparing the business plan for a lender, they will likely have specific requirements for this section. Some commonly included information might include resumes of your key management and owners as well as personal financial statements of the owners. You'll also need to include copies of important legal documents about your business and IRS registration documents showing your federal corporate taxpayer ID number. Any other information that may be helpful to your readers such as copies of patents or building and equipment leases may also be included.

No matter what type of business plan you write, whether formal or summary, keep in mind that the document is only a summary of your research. You must still conduct the business planning activity no matter what type of business plan document you prepare.

Part 6: Resources

"A room without books is like a body without a soul."

—Cicero

Templates @ BusinessStratup101.com

Personal Financial Statement
Market Matrix
Income Statement
Cash Flow

All worksheets included in Business Start-up 101 can be found in
a full sized document, available for download at
www.BusinessStart-up101.com.

Selected Titles by Michael E. Gerber

	The Most Successful Small Business in the World: The Ten Principles
	The E-Myth Mastery: The Seven Essential Disciplines for Building a World Class Company
	The E-Myth Enterprise: How to Turn a Great Idea into a Thriving Business
	Awakening the Entrepreneur Within: How Ordinary People Can Create Extraordinary Companies

www.MichaelEGerber.com

Chris Gattis

Chris started what is now Blue Point Strategies, LLC, a business consultancy, in 1984. He works with business owners who are struggling with the business part of running a business. From start-ups to turnarounds, Chris works with owners of small business to develop strategies and systems to allow owners to achieve the financial success that drove them into business in the first place. Blue Point Strategies offers workshops, classes, and one-on-one coaching to assist business owners in achieving their dreams.

He has a background in corporate finance and operations serving in various direct capacities including CFO of the nation's largest privately-held insulation and construction products distributor, credit manager for the US division of a multi-national construction products manufacturer and director of a small plastics manufacturing business. He has over 27 years of successful experience managing start-ups and turnarounds of large and small businesses as well as financial analysis, budget formulation, strategic planning, team building and risk management. Chris has managed small businesses, wrestled with unreasonable demands from banks and struggled with cash flow to make payroll. He understands the needs of and demands on small business owners.

Chris started his consulting career as a real estate appraiser focusing on income, commercial and industrial properties. He has held a Certified General Real Estate Appraiser license in Alabama and Indiana. His consulting experiences range from advising individual clients on real estate financing and development activities, managing start-ups and turnarounds of small businesses and site selection and expansion activities with a major Japanese automaker and Tier 1 auto suppliers.

He has served on local planning and zoning commissions and development authorities giving him an insight and understanding of dealing with local cities and towns to further his clients' needs. In addition to his consulting practice, Chris serves as a business coach for a local entrepreneurial development center, an instructor for an area technical college and a keynote speaker.

Blue Point Strategies, LLC
Huntsville, Alabama
www.BluePointStrategies.com
cgattis@BluePointStrategies.com

www.BusinessStart-up101.com

Made in the USA
Lexington, KY
05 August 2016